Thoughtful and gently written, *Hunting for Honey* invites readers into an encounter with God's nearness. With each chapter, you'll start noticing His fingerprints in the ordinary and extraordinary alike. You won't just read about God's love; you'll begin to recognize it in your own life. It's tender, honest, and quietly transformational-in all the best ways.

Bob Goff, author of four *NY Times* bestsellers, including *Love Does*.

Hunting
for
HONEY

HEIDI GIANNI

Hunting
for
HONEY

Seeking GOD in the
Everyday and Unexpected

Cover design by Vanessa Mendozzi
Interior design by KUHN Design Group

ISBNs
Paperback: 979-8-9930317-0-5
Hardcover (dust): 979-8-9930317-2-9
Hardcover (case): 979-9-9930317-1-2
eBook: 979-8-9930317-3-6

Library of Congress Control Number: 2025919349

Printed in the United States of America

To you,
the one who wonders
if God really sees, loves, and cares,
like I did.

My prayer is that you find
what your heart and soul
are longing for.

CONTENTS

INTRODUCTION

I used to think God was only for people who had everything fig-ured out. For the people who never doubted His timing, calling, and leading. I knew that God was real, but I didn't know that He cared about the details of my life, let alone me, personally. But then something shifted.

It happened when I finally gave up, throwing my hands up in frustration (and shedding a few tears of pure sadness) over my for-ever-single situation, stuck in yet another cycle of dead-end dating. During that time, I whispered a tiny prayer, asking God to help me. I never imagined He was actually listening.

And, oh boy, did He hear me.

For this particular prayer, God's answer didn't happen overnight or instantly. There was no tall, dark, and handsome man who was teleported onto my doorstep that next morning. But instead, God answered through a series of small things, all working together for my good, to write the most beautiful love story of my life.

These tiny moments from God felt like little drops of honey. They were sweet, surprising, and enough to make me wonder: *What if God is really there? Is He on my side? Did He hear my whisper of desperation?*

If you're skeptical or unsure about God and what He might be doing in your life, I get it; I've been there. Or maybe you know God, but want to know Him better—to be closer to Him and deepen your relationship with Him. Here's the thing: What if you just start looking for those drops of honey in your daily life? What if there's more sweetness in your life than you realize?

Maybe it's in the beauty of a pink and orange sunset, a red tulip popping out of the snow, or meeting a new friend or future spouse.

Thankfully, you don't need all the answers to start hunting for honey.

Just start where you are.

I'm excited for you to discover God's sweetness and His goodness in both the ordinary and the extraordinary moments of life. My hope is that you begin hunting for honey in your own story. I am sure you will find it…and will never look at life or God the same way again.

READER'S NOTE

In this book, I want to be completely real with you. I will share my deepest vulnerabilities, insecurities, and hardships, not to put the spotlight on me but to reveal how even in my most broken moments God showed up. Again and again, He proved to be the answer, the solution to my every cry, whenever I sought Him with all my heart.

You'll notice that the chapters in this book aren't woven together like a traditional story. Instead, they are stand-alone snapshots. They are my encounters with God written in the order they happened over the years. While you may see gaps of time between chapters, that's because this isn't a book about my life in every detail. It's a book about God, who He is, how He works, and how His presence has marked my journey.

My stories simply serve as the backdrop, the canvas on which His faithfulness is displayed. My hope is that as you read, you'll not only glimpse how He has met me in the everyday and the unexpected but that you'll also be encouraged to notice Him in your own story too.

At the end of each chapter, you will find a "Honey Nugget". These little treasures are drawn from God's Word, His character, and His faithfulness. They are meant to be savored slowly, like a sweet drop of honey that lingers, nourishes, and gives you a truth to hold onto. My hope is that you will return to them often, hold them close on both ordinary and difficult days, and let them remind you of who God is and how He is present in your story.

CHAPTER 1

MY BLIND DATE

I met my husband, Michael, on a blind date. I was twenty years old and in college at San Diego State University; he was twenty-four and had already graduated from SDSU the year before. My sorority, Kappa Alpha Theta, was hosting a dance where we needed to invite a date for the Hawaiian-themed night called Mai Tai Massacre. Everyone had some special guy in mind, except for a few of us. I was a recovering ex-girlfriend and coming up to breathe again after going through, at that time of my life, the worst experience of relationship pain I had ever known. Let's name him Heartbreak #1. (Spoiler alert: If I named that one #1, you know there is a #2.) I had put all my trust in this relationship and thought he would be my forever since he was my high school sweetheart. The devastating part was he did not think or feel the same way, having moved on to the next girl before we even broke up, which left me spiraling for a long time.

I questioned the two and a half years we were together and every decision we had made. What was hard was sharing our high school memories and then both of us attending the same college where running into each other happened all too frequently. I wanted to crawl into a hole and never see him, but I did. Being on the same campus and in the Greek system, our paths collided often. It was nearly impossible to not see him, and when I did see him, it would throw me for a loop. I know I spent more time recovering than I should have from our breakup. This was also the first time I experienced heartbreak; it felt like a distinct, sharp, searing pain that engulfed my chest. The mental anguish was equally intense, like a storm raging inside my mind. Seeing my ex with other girls sent an army of negative thoughts and lies I began to believe about myself. I felt lost and vulnerable, far too young and naive to handle the weight of the emotional turmoil on my own. The deep wounds our breakup left behind felt like they had severed not only my heart but also my very sense of self. My identity was left crushed due to the new reality of realizing our future together was over.

Anyway, back to my dance... Mai Tai Massacre, my sorority's highly anticipated annual event, was fast approaching, and I needed a date. Since the dance's theme was Hawaiian, we spent an obscene amount of time getting our outfits ready for the big night, but let's be real; that was half the fun! I wore a pair of black Levi's® jean shorts that fit me perfectly, paired with a colorful pink floral button-down shirt. The shirt had intricate details of vibrant flowers that contrasted beautifully against the black shorts. To complete the look, I slipped into a pair of cute, little white sandals that added (what I thought at the time) a touch of elegance to the casual ensemble. It was 1991, so, of course, I crimped my hair almost to the point of singeing it off and pulled the front half up in a pink scrunchie on top of my head, finishing it off with an ozone-depleting amount of hairspray—perfect.

A group of us rented a limo that drove to pick up all of our dates, who had gathered at my date's house to "get ready" for the dance party. My big sis in the sorority set me up with her good guy friend, and the guys were all outside to greet us as we pulled up to his house off 63rd Street near our university.

That was the moment I saw my date, Michael Gianni, for the first time: He was so handsome. The first thing I noticed was that he was remarkably tall, towering over everyone around him. His hair was a sun-kissed shade of blondish-brown, meticulously coiffed into a perfect side-sweeping part that seemed to catch the sunlight just right. As the stretch limousine pulled in, his face lit up with the most charming, radiant smile that seemed to stretch from ear to ear. Of course, all of us girls had to stand up and stick our heads out the sunroof as we pulled up to make sure they noticed us too! It's so funny now when I think back on the memory and the life we have now.

I was a bit nervous to meet this "older guy" but quickly felt comfortable in his presence upon meeting. He was easy to be with, quite the conversationalist, and exactly what I needed! The night ended up being a lot of fun and the first time in a while that I had forgotten about my single situation. After that Hawaiian night, Michael and I saw each other casually for a few months. We never got super serious; we just had friendly, fun dates over the long, warm summer months in San Diego.

In the fall, my sorority hosted another big dance known as Perfect Match. This time, we joined with another sorority, and it turned out to be the event of the season where couples would dress in matching T-shirts and jeans or coordinate outfits that were creative to represent the theme. It was such a popular dance that you could sense the anticipation and excitement among all the college guys as the event approached! They came out of the woodwork, hoping to be invited and be the "perfect match" for one of the sorority girls, who had to ask the guys to the dance to begin with. I invited Michael. We wore matching dark green T-shirts and blue Levi's® jeans. It was simple, but we looked cute and like a perfect match.

But how exactly did I feel about our relationship? Do you know how it feels when the dentist numbs your mouth and you can't feel your tongue or the slobber dripping down your chin? Or when you sleep on your arm wrong and you can't lift it no matter how hard you try and you have no feeling for a while after? So with our relationship, I felt numb, waiting to feel something. Not how I should have felt, especially with how fabulously Michael always treated me. I felt guilty and sad and not myself.

We both enjoyed each other's company, but with no explanation and with no hard feelings, we went our separate ways. Our attraction and contact simply and slowly dwindled off, to the point where we stopped calling each other and the dates stopped. I was an immature junior in college, still finding my way and, sadly, still heartbroken and mourning my last relationship. Michael was a young adult doing all the adult things, holding down a job, traveling for work, buying cars, etc. He was out in the world, while I had no idea what in the world I wanted to do.

That was the first time we dated.

For the next five years, we saw each other maybe two or three times at various events, being friendly but nothing more. There were no hard feelings between us. We would hug and say hello and be on our way until one night in the Gaslamp Quarter in downtown San Diego. Something changed when we literally ran into each other on the street corner. Was it a coincidence? Right timing? Serendipity? God? Or all of the above?

Now, years later, I firmly believe it was God aligning our paths.

God's plan for our relationship had many moving parts: His friends insisted they go downtown that night, of all nights; both of us were single; my brother had to drag me out of the house to even go out. None of these were coincidences; all of them could have and should have not happened. God coordinated this, our "running into each other." I give Him all the credit and glory, especially now that I sit here years later, remembering the beginning.

I talked to Michael on the street corner while his friends, my brother, and all of my brother's friends waited.

"How are you? Where are you working? Where are you living?"

All the casual catch-up questions were asked and answered by us during that time. It had probably been two years since I had seen him, but it felt like it was yesterday, and I hadn't moved on from my previous breakup yet. Seeing Michael and hearing about what he was up to was fun. The way his eyes lit up as he recounted his adventures was endearing, and I remembered how much I enjoyed talking to him. Then, what he did next shocked me. He leaned into me with genuine curiosity; his eyes fixated on my left hand's ring finger, which was crossed over my arm because I was freezing and doing everything possible to stay warm that December night.

"So, are you married?" he casually asked.

Hmmm, wow! I thought to myself. No guy had ever asked me that before. "No," I remember saying with immediate flashbacks to my recent breakup. I was single for all of one month. I thought my life was OVER, and I would be forgotten, a spinster to my dying day. I was only there because my brother Drew had forced me to go out that night and would not take no for an answer; otherwise, I would have stayed home, wallowing in self-pity. Thanks to Drew, that was the night that changed my life.

Seeing Michael again was different this time because we said we would stay in touch and planned to see each other sometime soon. After running into each other on that street corner, we kept walking in opposite directions down the busy street. I was so excited to see him, but my heart was still wrapped up and mourning my last relationship, Heartbreak #2. Yes, I know, I did it again. It's so unfortunate, but I put my trust in another guy who could not commit to save his life! How had I picked another unfaithful, unloyal guy? I was 0 for 2 and feeling really down and out. My "guy picker" was off, to say the least. Between the two relationships, I had literally wasted five years of my life, not counting the years it took me to get over them.

The jury is still out if Heartbreak #2 was worse than #1, but I was in it again. Rejection, loss, and hopelessness were becoming far too common in my dating life. No wonder there are so many songs about heartbreak; it is a real thing that paralyzes you like a venomous snake, slowly squeezing the life out of its prey. I seriously felt like I was about to die after the second guy said no to committing to me. He loved me and wanted me to be his wife, but he could not commit. We had been dating for two-and-a-half years, and we were twenty-five and twenty-eight years old, so this was no young high school fling like last time. It was real and supposed to lead to the next step and last forever. Instead, I had given up so much of myself to make it work, and it still didn't work. It was devastating.

I kept myself very distracted at the time with my job. I was teaching first grade, and the little five- and six-year-olds were the joy of my life. They made me smile every moment I was with them during the school day when I couldn't manage to crack a grin all the other hours of the day. Like in the movies, I held on to the unreal expectation that my former boyfriend would change his mind. Like a knight in shining armor, he would come galloping into town on a white horse, drop to one knee, and beg me to be his wife. He would then swoop me up onto the back of the stallion (with one hand because the other was holding the bejeweled sword), and we would ride into the sunset. Sadly, he did not do that. Day after day, I waited for him, but he never came. But God was up to something because this was when I ran into my college blind date from five years before.

What I was unaware of at the time was the evening that Michael and I ran into each other in the Gaslamp Quarter, he had an interesting conversation that very evening up in Los Angeles before he drove down to San Diego. Michael's aunt and stepmom had probed and prodded him about the women in his life, something we females love to do.

So the God thing is this: Michael is the catch of all catches, yet somehow, no woman had captured his heart until that night. There were close ones, but none stuck. He was a young professional working across the US and Europe, building his knowledge and expertise over the prior five years as a consultant for wireless operators building out their mobile networks. His aunt and stepmom continued the relationship interrogation by asking him, "If you could marry any one of the ladies you dated, who would it be?" Later, he told me he didn't even have to think about it and said my name at the time: Heidi Kleis. Do you have chills? Because I do!

The exact night we "ran into each other," Michael had answered the question of whom he would marry if he could marry anyone, and he picked me. A girl he hadn't dated in five years but was about to run into on a street corner that very night.

This example is to show God is always at work, whether we see it or not, whether we acknowledge it or not. He is a master planner, and He sees it all.

I will guide you along the best pathway for your
life. I will advise you and watch over you.
PSALM 32:8 NLT

The Lord was at work, and I hadn't seen it yet. I was clueless, heartbroken, and blinded from my previous relationship, but the Lord knew. He saw me and my heart. He knew Michael and his heart. Michael knew the Lord and was seeking the Lord's direction and help at that time; for me, I was clueless at the time about God leading me to Michael. We both have to wonder if our short-lived relationship hadn't fizzled out five years prior, what our life would have been like. It would have been so different. But you know what? It is fine to wonder, but I would never question how it turned out.

Now I look back and see that God had a plan for Michael and me, and it could not be defined by anyone. Let me ask you: Are you going through heartbreak yourself? Are you questioning how things worked out in your life? I don't know exactly where you are, but God does. He is a good God and a good Father to us, His children, loving us more than anything.

I would have lost heart, unless I had believed that I would
see the goodness of the Lord in the land of the living.
PSALM 27:13

Soon after that meeting on the street corner, we started dating casually for a few months. He lived in LA, and I lived in San Diego, so we saw each other for some fun weekend dates—going out to dinner or a street fair in Pacific Beach. It was casual and fun and helped me to ignore a big problem still in my heart. I was still heartbroken and full of pain. My heart was not healthy because I was so wrapped up in my ex potentially coming back, so I could not see Michael or our relationship clearly. I was blind, so blind to the amazing, handsome, God-loving man standing right in front of me, doting over me, taking me out for amazing meals and conversation. I literally could not see him for who he was sitting across from me at the table. So we broke up, with me initiating the breakup.

That was the second time we dated.

Fast forward to the end of summer in 1997 when I worked on my master's degree while elementary school was out for summer vacation and was swamped with schoolwork. I felt like I was at an emotional breaking point with my love life as well, discouraged, sad, and oh so alone. Have you heard the saying, "Always a bridesmaid, never a bride"? That was me. The term was coined after me. Okay, maybe not just me. Maybe you too?

At that time, I had been in eight weddings and had all the dresses to prove it. The movie *27 Dresses* had a few more than me, but you get the picture. I was at my wit's end. Finally, I surrendered control to God for the very first time in my life, hoping He was listening and cared enough to answer me. I said a very simple prayer that I believe the Lord took and answered by softening my heart and opening my eyes. I had hit rock bottom on the guy front, so the prayer I said was something like:

> *God, will You help me because I can't find a guy to marry. I am lost, and I am so tired of trying to find him. I need Your help!*

I know it sounds pathetic and desperate, but I was. I needed the Lord in my life so badly and had finally sought Him instead of trying to figure it out on my own. I am telling you this because God loves it when we tell Him the truth and give it to Him. I knew God, but I didn't *KNOW* God. (Does that make sense?) I knew of Him and knew a bunch of memorized prayers but never saw any answered prayers, or God, for that matter. I thought God was watching my every move and couldn't wait to punish me, like a little kid zapping an ant with a magnifying glass. I am unsure how you see God, but it will change your life if you understand who He is, what His character is like, and what we mean to Him. I was so wrong in who I thought God was, thinking He was an all-knowing scorekeeper and punisher. Instead, I found out He is my loving Father. This is where my perspective and understanding started; it was life-changing in how I view God now.

Before this surrender, I purposely ignored my heart and my feelings for Michael and our breakup until my birthday. Something happened. I felt it happen. Michael sent me a birthday card and used black and red ink interchangeably to write it. He used red ink to write *Happy Birthday Heidi* and black ink for the rest, then in red ink he wrote, *Love, Michael.* And then he drew a red heart by his name. I can still see it in my mind. He had also included pictures of us together that we had taken the last few months we were together in the card. I sat reading the card and looking at the photographs of us, thinking, *Man, he was so kind, and why hadn't I seen it until now?* It was all there in the pictures. Michael was such a good man. He never pushed me to be physical and cared for and treated me like I was lovely. I had never been treated that way before by anyone. My heart was melting, and at that moment, my heart turned toward Michael, where it has been ever since. I was falling for him, but remember, we were broken up, again. So I needed to mend the relationship and win him back. I knew something was up with me because I was suddenly so nervous when I picked up the phone to thank him for the card. I had never felt that way with him before.

Third time's the charm.

Well, no charm here. This was the Lord working and softening and aligning our hearts and lives for the most magnificent life ahead. This is when my relationship with God began to be more real as well. I felt like He was working in my life, and I could see it happening before my eyes. He is and always has been on the throne! I want you to know He also hears you. He hears and cares. He had a story for my life that was unfolding before me and has the same for you too.

Looking back on these events, both Michael and I finding and seeing God, reminds me so much of the Scripture from Romans.

And we know that all things work together for good to those who love God, to those who are the called according to His purpose.
Romans 8:28

or

That's why we can be so sure that every detail in our lives of love for God is worked into something good.
Romans 8:28 msg

God is at work in ALL things! He took my anguish and made it good, so good. He took the ashes of my life, which felt like death, darkness, and despair, and turned them into something beautiful that I could have never imagined. He is a good God who loved me, helped me, and gave me a husband who far exceeded my expectations.

Now to Him who is able to do exceedingly abundantly above all
that we ask or think, according to the power that works in us.
EPHESIANS 3:20

My blind date turned into my Perfect Match, and then my husband, my Ephesians 3:20 man. It was like God was showing off by giving me a man who was even more than I could ever think or imagine! I was frail and untrusting because of the uncommitted men from my past, but who would God have for me? The strongest, most grounded, most loving man who couldn't wait to get married and be committed to his wife, that's who. Michael had the exact opposite character of the two men I had previously picked. This only shows God was on the throne, and I was beginning to see that God was real and trustworthy, changing everything about my life.

HONEY NUGGET

Even in heartbreak's deepest shadows, God
is quietly weaving a story far greater than we
can imagine, one of love, redemption, and
blessings beyond our wildest dreams.

CHAPTER 2

MARRY ME

I love that God is at work in our lives, even when we fail to see Him. That truth of His faithfulness is profound—constant, unwavering, unchanged yesterday, today, and tomorrow.

Even when Michael and I were broken up and I was blind and unaware of God's work in my life, He was at work! He loved Michael and heard his prayers during the summer that we had broken up. I later learned my husband was so upset about our second break up that he started praying next to his bed on his knees every morning! He was faithfully seeking God's help and direction, and God answered Michael's prayers for our relationship to be restored if it was His will. Remember how I mentioned that something happened to my heart toward Michael? I truly believe that Michael's prayers changed everything for us. God heard him and softened my heart toward Michael and opening my eyes to who he really was. I was no longer blind to the treasure in front of me.

Michael and I had been on the fast track with our relationship after we decided to start dating a third time. Within six months, we were engaged. Everything seemed so easy, and the next steps came so naturally. This was also the first healthy and thriving relationship either of us had been in with zero game-playing involved, unlike previous relationships. From the moment we started dating for the third time, we quickly progressed to saying "I love you" and "I want to spend the rest of my life with you." We had so much fun dating during this time; it was one of the happiest times of my life so far.

Once I released my ex from my heart, I was healthy again; everything made sense with Michael. He was a dream boyfriend, and I was the luckiest girl on earth! I say lucky because at the time I thought I was lucky: lucky to have been set up with him, lucky he liked me, and lucky he was my boyfriend. Looking back, I now realize this was not luck but rather a blessing and favor from the Lord. Everything good comes from God, and our relationship was no exception.

Our path to being engaged after six years of dating could be made into a movie! I am not kidding; it was spectacular! I wouldn't have changed a thing about it! Michael did everything right and made me feel like I had never felt before, truly loved for who I was and that I was worth it.

At that time, I had plans to visit a dear friend, Heather (another sorority sister), over a three-day weekend in March. We were going to visit her quaint, beautiful town of Marin, California, and had made plans for a great girls' weekend. She surprised me with a big dinner on Saturday night in downtown San Francisco at the award-winning, world-famous Carnelian Room on the fifty-second floor of the Bank of America building. I was so excited to go with her that night. While I was packing, Michael was helping me pick out what to wear to this event, choosing a long black and white floral silky skirt and a thin black sweater. I loved that he helped me pack for the trip, not suspecting a thing.

He took me to the airport and got me to the gate; this was during a time when non-passengers were still allowed to enter the terminals. We said our goodbyes, and I told him that I would see him on Monday night. Once I arrived in Marin, my friend and I had the best time that weekend! She had the cutest apartment, and her neighborhood was filled with little cafes, lunch spots, and fun shops.

On Saturday afternoon, we quickly changed and hopped into the car to get to dinner in "the city," which was an hour away. Upon arrival, we parked and took the elevator to the top floor of the tall highrise! The view was spectacular with the city and the bay spread out below us. The sky was glowing as the sun was about to set. Once we were seated, we saw the maître d' had seated us facing the city, and we giggled with excitement. I told Heather how grateful I was that she invited me, and soon after she excused herself to the bathroom. As I admired the view, the maître d' returned and handed me a beautifully wrapped gift and a letter.

Confused, I looked around for Heather, but she had not yet returned. I opened the letter and was surprised to find the most beautiful, romantic love letter from Michael, expressing his love for me. I kept looking up for my friend's return so I could share the moment with her. When I opened the box, I found a bottle of the perfume Michael had given me when we first started dating when I turned twenty-one, Romeo De Romeo Gigli. The scent instantly transported me back to those early years, and I was overwhelmed with love and emotion. It was surreal, and I didn't know if I was having an out-of-body experience because our relationship seemed too good to be true at that moment.

When I looked up, I was shocked to see Michael standing beside me, reaching for my hand. My mind could not comprehend what was happening. I kept saying, "What are you doing here?", unable to process the situation calmly. Thinking on this now, I wish I had worn something a little less teacherish and had said something other than, "What are you doing here?" Lol.

Michael was wearing a tailored, navy blue crew neck shirt, a coordinating sports coat, meticulously pressed pants, a matching belt, and perfectly shined shoes. He looked dapper. I remember wondering to myself why he was dressed so nicely. Then it happened, answering my question and satisfying every desire of my heart—he slowly bent down on one knee. Michael looked up at me, his eyes locked on mine, and he said that he had found the one he wanted to spend the rest of his life with, loving me more than he ever thought possible. He said I was the answer to his prayers and he knew God had brought me back to him. Next, he said gently, "Heidi, will you be my wife that I will love and adore for all of our lives?"

Now I was having a hands-down, out-of-body experience. The most intense heat wave rolled over my body as I sat in disbelief. My brain could not stop firing questions at me as my eyes tried to focus and my ears strained to hear what Michael was saying to me from one knee. Was it actually me this man was talking to? Was it finally my turn to answer the question I had been waiting and dreaming of my entire life? Was this the man I would spend the rest of my life with: every day, every night, every hardship, every celebration? And oh my goodness, was this the man I would be saying yes to so we would have children together?

I could not process all that was flooding my mind and the excitement I could not contain! My head was exploding, and my body was on fire. All I had to do was answer him with a yes, and everything I had ever wanted would be real. Thankfully, I couldn't say yes fast enough as I lunged toward him to embrace my new fiancé! The entire restaurant clapped, and the wait staff, dressed in tuxedos, began to serve us champagne and the most decadent meal I had ever eaten. We talked and kissed throughout the meal. Our eyes were locked on each other, and I felt so surreal. I was engaged to the man of my dreams!

However, that is not the end of the story. After dinner Michael said we were going to the Tom Hopkins Hotel for a drink at the bar. I was on cloud nine. Reality started to set in that I had the most handsome man next to me who just asked me to be his wife. I also had a beautiful diamond ring on my finger that I never thought would be there. Both he and the ring were exceeding any expectation of mine. My mind was taking it all in, and it felt like I was watching someone else's life unfold before me.

On the drive over in a taxi, I wanted to call my mom and dad as I couldn't wait to tell them the news! They were the first call I had to make. I was close to my mom; she knew everything happening in my life. She was my best friend and biggest fan as she loved me and was so supportive and encouraging. I wanted to be just like her when I was little, for she was a wife, mom, and teacher, which became my dream too. Michael redirected my request to call them by saying we were almost at the hotel and could call them then.

Once at the bar we were seated at another beautiful table overlooking the city. It was already dark, and the sparkling lights were breathtaking. We ordered our drinks and continued to talk about our love and the best surprise of my lifetime. A few minutes later, our drinks were delivered, but who delivered them? My parents! I screamed with delight as my mom set down my drink, and my dad set down Michael's. Michael had flown up to San Francisco with my parents that morning. Are you kidding me? What a plan! He knew how much my parents meant to me and how special it would be to have them there. By then, the live music had started, so we all walked out to the dance floor to join Heather, her boyfriend, and a few of their friends, all in on the surprise. My sweet friend Heather had been in on the surprise for weeks with Michael. She was like a professional event planner the way she helped orchestrate all the big and little details of the weekend, fully convincing me that the company that she worked for had given her a monster gift certificate for her outstanding work and she wanted me to join her to enjoy this celebration dinner while I was there. I believed every word she said. It became a true celebration, and we danced the night away.

So how did he pull it all off? Michael had planned the entire weekend out to a T. Remember I said that we drove an hour from my friend's apartment to the city? Michael had arranged a hotel room for my parents and me and a room for himself to stay after the proposal. But what about the logistics of me staying in the city when all my stuff was at my friend's house in Marin, you ask? Well, Michael and my sister Gretchen had gone shopping the week before and bought me everything I would need to stay in the city. He bought me pajamas, green corduroy overalls with a white long-sleeved shirt, even underwear, a bra, makeup, a hairbrush, hair clips, shoes, absolutely everything I would need for that night and the next day! The love I felt was something I hadn't experienced before. Was this guy for real?

The next day, my parents, Michael, and I walked around the city and enjoyed touring the hot spots—Fisherman's Wharf, Ghirardelli Chocolate, and Chinatown. We had the most memorable day with the four of us. It truly was so special and thoughtful, and I was beyond excited and still in shock that it was truly happening. I looked at Michael a million times, overthinking how **lucky** I was and how I didn't deserve such a great guy who loved me so well.

HONEY NUGGET

God is always at work, weaving love and blessing into our lives in ways we can't yet see until one day His plan unfolds and we realize it's been His goodness all along.

CHAPTER 3

I HAVE WAITED FOR YOU FOR SO LONG

I had dreamed of being a wife for as long as I could remember, and I knew I needed a good husband. No, not just a good husband, a great, godly, committed husband who would ALSO be a great dad. However, it was quite daunting to look at the list of attributes my future husband needed to have. I had a horrible time finding the perfect match on my own before Michael came along. I had to ask God for help, and He showed me He was good and trustworthy when He gave me Michael. Dream met.

Thank you, Lord!

The second phase of my dream was to be a mom. We did not waste any time in that area of life, and I got pregnant during our honeymoon. Eeeek! We were so surprised! We were only married for a few weeks when we discovered that we weren't only newlyweds but also expectant parents. It was so exciting and scary at the same time, happening so quickly and so easily! I am sure there were a few people we knew who rolled their eyes at our fast pace and also counted the months after our wedding, especially because our first baby arrived three weeks early. God, Michael, and I knew the truth, and we were elated! It felt surreal to me to be married and pregnant.

> *For I know the thoughts that I think toward*
> *you, says the Lord, thoughts of peace and not*
> *of evil, to give you a future and a hope.*
> JEREMIAH 29:11

The first weekend home from our honeymoon (before we knew we were pregnant), we started attending a new church, a non-denominational church that Michael had been to a few times. The worship and the teaching were incredible. After church, we ran into a bunch of Michael's long-time friends in the courtyard. One couple had a brand-new baby girl, and the other friend had a tow-headed, energetic two-year-old son. I ogled over the newborn, and Michael played on the grass with the toddler. We drove home, saying how sweet and fun they were and how someday we would be parents too. That was a setup; I am sure of it now, knowing how the days unfolded for us in the following weeks.

I suspected something was up and not normal because my "Aunt Flo" (women, you know who I am talking about) was not coming for her monthly visit as expected. I told Michael that morning as I walked out the door to work. He jumped into action and went to the store for a pregnancy test while I taught school that day. It was a few days before I realized "she" was late. I was so busy with wedding gifts and thank-you notes, seeing our friends, and getting back into a routine after our honeymoon. But after realizing she was missing, I was on high alert. All day at school, I expected her untimely arrival, but she didn't arrive. At recess, lunch break, and after school, no visiting relative. I could barely keep my focus that day, teaching with my mind elsewhere. Was I pregnant?

At the time, I was a first-grade teacher at a school in California, my dream job, and had started work on a master's degree at San Diego State University in curriculum and instruction.

Later that day, I got home from school and made dinner for my new husband. It was so much fun! I was so excited to see him every night. To this day, dinner is a much anticipated time of day when we reconnect and share with each other about our day. After dinner, I took the test and left it on the counter in the bathroom. Michael went to look at the results as I asked him to be part of this special chapter. After a few minutes, he walked out of the bathroom and said, "Sweet cheeks, we are having a baby!" I fell back onto the couch with tears of joy streaming uncontrollably from my face.

God, did You know this? Did You plan this? This is too good to be true!

I was in disbelief because how in the world had both my lifelong dreams not only happened but were also beyond what I could have ever thought or imagined and all in the same month! It seemed unreal and too good to be true—a husband and pregnant, all in October 1998!

Just over a year before this, I was living in despair and sadness, and now I was living the dream I had had since my third birthday when my parents gave me my first baby doll. My faith was so new, and I was so curious about God. I had so many questions! Was He the One who was orchestrating this all together for my good? I was keenly aware there was a change, but I couldn't quite put my finger on it. At this point, I didn't fully understand that God was on my side or that He was good. I found this Scripture that answered my question.

> *So, what do you think? With God on our side like this,*
> *how can we lose? If God didn't hesitate to put everything*
> *on the line for us, embracing our condition and exposing*
> *himself to the worst by sending his own Son, is there*
> *anything else he would gladly and freely do for us?*
> ROMANS 8:31-32 MSG

So many good things were happening in my life. I was curious if they were from God, luck, or timing? Just like I questioned earlier when Michael and I ran into each other on the street corner in downtown San Diego. I was watching with eyes wide open. I had been learning so much, not only about the Bible but also about the Father God, His Son, Jesus Christ, and the works of the Holy Spirit. I found the most beautiful answers to my questions regarding who God was and what He thought of us, which I share in the verses below.

> *For the Lord is good; his steadfast love endures forever,*
> *and his faithfulness to all generations.*
> PSALM 100:5 ESV

> *How precious to me are your thoughts,*
> *O God! How vast is the sum of them!*
> PSALM 139:17 ESV

But God shows his love for us in that while
we were still sinners, Christ died for us.

ROMANS 5:8 ESV

So we have come to know and to believe the love
that God has for us. God is love, and whoever abides
in love abides in God, and God abides in him.

1 JOHN 4:16 ESV

Just as he chose us in Him before the foundation
of the world, that we should be holy and without
blame before Him in love, having predestined
us to adoption as sons by Jesus Christ to Himself,
according to the good pleasure of His will.

EPHESIANS 1:4-5

See what kind of love the Father has given to
us, that we should be called children of God;
and so we are. The reason why the world does
not know us is that it did not know him.

1 JOHN 3:1 ESV

God absolutely loves us and is only good. It was so hard to wrap my mind around this new truth, but this is where everything changes. It all changes when we realize God is good. He is loving. He is on our side and loved us before we even knew Him. God delights in us and has great plans for us. It all starts with a faith journey and truly believing and trusting God.

God loves us. God loves you. God loves me.

In Trust by Henry Cloud, Cloud explains that trust is built by a person feeling understood. "Trust allows us to know that 'this person knows me. This person knows what I am feeling, what I want, what matters to me,' and more."[1]

I began to trust God because I began to see that God was working in my life and He understood me and saw me. This is what changed everything in my life. This is what I want for you too, to know God and how much He loves you and that He can be trusted. I want this so much for you that I have written all of these stories for you to see Him. So what changed my perspective of Him? My understanding is what changed: me, not God. He had been there all these years, lovingly watching me and waiting for me to come to Him and understand who He was, His character, and His intentions. I needed to understand His character and unending love before I could trust Him.

Behold, I stand at the door and knock, if anyone
hears My voice and opens the door, I will come in
to him and dine with him and he with Me.

REVELATION 3:20

I didn't have much of a faith journey before this specific time in my life because I didn't realize, believe, or accept that God loved me unconditionally and to the absolutely highest degree of never-ending, to infinity and beyond, to the moon and back, and more than I could wrap my mind or heart around that kind of love. I just couldn't fathom it.

God's love for us is unshakable, and His love will move mountains, stop storms, heal wounded hearts, transform lives, and free those who are held captive by shame and sin. His love is powerful and working. I was seeing His love in my life like never before. He heard and saw me. He loved me, and my understanding of this literally changed everything about my life.

Fast forward seven months, I was thirty-four weeks pregnant and teaching my amazing little first graders one day when my belly kept contracting; I know now they are called Braxton Hicks. They are sporadic contractions and relaxation of the uterine muscle and can also be called false labor. After school, I called the doctor, and they said, "Oh, don't worry, that is normal. We will check you at your next appointment." I know I was a first-time mom, but I had this strange feeling that things were not normal, so I advocated for myself and asked to please get me into the office that day, May 18, 1999. I know this date because it was the last day I ever taught school. I HAD no idea this would be my final day at school, but God did.

The doctor admitted me to the hospital immediately where I stayed for the next week, and then they let me go home on bed rest.

After almost four weeks of bed rest, I reached thirty-seven weeks. The doctors said if I could make it that far, then I could get up as that is the week when babies are no longer considered preemies but full-term. That day could not come fast enough! I made it, and that first day off of bed rest, I ran a million errands, including driving my car and getting outside my house! I had a mile-long to-do list that I had made while lying in bed with my mind racing and preparing for this little baby to arrive. Michael and I met for a quick lunch at UTC (University Town Center) and walked around in the warm sunshine. That night we went to dinner with friends and the movies. I was in a bit of shock being out and about and seeing so many people and the hustle and bustle of life that I had missed during the last month. I had really hard contractions during the movie, but I thought it was because we saw the action-packed *Star Wars I: The Phantom Menace.*

We climbed into bed just after 11 p.m., and by 2 a.m., I was up. My water had broken.

Let me just say a million little things had to happen to get me to that point. The one dream I longed for and dreamed of my entire life was hours away from happening. I longed to hold my baby, see my baby, and smother my baby in kisses and tender love. I will spare you all the gory details of what happened next, but after hard labor and forty torturous minutes after the baby was born and checked out by a specialty team, I FINALLY got to hold him. They set him on my chest, and the first thing I said to him was, "I have waited for you for so long."

All my dreams had come true. I loved him more than I ever thought was possible. My husband stood beside me with the biggest, proudest smile and kissed me as we looked at this beautiful baby boy, Jake. He was a product of our love and God's goodness, a gift from the Lord.

> *Every good gift and every perfect gift is from above,*
> *and comes down from the Father of lights.*
> **JAMES 1:17**

I had waited for twenty-eight years for June 11, 1999, to have my deepest desire and dream come true. I wasn't alone in the waiting. It seems to be a recurring theme here on earth. Did you know that Joseph in the Bible waited thirteen years for his dream, Abraham waited twenty-five years, Moses waited forty years, and Jesus waited thirty years? In case you thought you were alone in the waiting, you are not. God is at work, and there is a reason we have to wait for His changes to come through. Embrace it and wait well for your dream. The waiting is hard, frustrating, and long. Ask God what He wants us to learn and press into Him. Stop asking, "Why is this happening to me?" And stop comparing yourself to everyone else and their stories; this will only lead to bitterness and anxiety. God does not waste time. God has a plan, and He knows. He sees you. He knows the waiting is hard, but you are not alone. He is with you through it all. Let Him lead you and guide you. In my twenty-eight-year wait, God knew and He gets all the glory for the biggest, little six-pound dream I ever had, my little Jake.

HONEY NUGGET

The seasons we spend waiting in faith become the soil where God grows our most beautiful dreams.

CHAPTER 4

NO GREATER LOVE

I was head over heels with my first son, Jake. I could almost eat him;
I loved him so much! At the time, I was a busy, little bee taking
care of him and finding a new balance of all my priorities in life. I
loved being a mom and wife and was never happier. I am not saying
motherhood was easy at all; it was difficult and tiring, but I was so
in love with my new role.

What I noticed was this new love I had for my newborn. I had
never felt love like this before. I loved my parents, siblings, and ador-
ing husband, but my love for Jake was different. I didn't care what he
did, how many times he woke me up at night, how much spit-up he
launched, or how he cried at every red light when the car stopped.

I was crazy in love with him.

I wondered if the new crazy love I had was real. Did my parents
feel this way about me, their child? Was I experiencing parental love,
and did other parents feel this way too? Did God love us like that, love
everyone like that? He is God the Father, so did He love me like that?

My insecurities made that question harder to answer. Was I worth it? I have done so many stupid things in my life. Did He still love me?

For God so loved the world that He gave His
only begotten Son, that whoever believes in Him
should not perish and have everlasting life.
JOHN 3:16

This shift in my heart and new understanding of love began to slowly transform my life completely because I began to understand who God was and believe that He was trustworthy. I was able to see Him as a loving and good God and that His motives were right. He was for me, helping me with my life and all the circumstances. What helped me understand His great love more was this question:

What if I had to sacrifice Jake in the same way God sacrificed Jesus?

I thought about it for not even a second, "No!" I couldn't do it and wouldn't do it. I had waited for Jake for so long that I couldn't give him away like that. But as I wrestled with this comparison, I began to touch on how much God loved me. God DID sacrifice Jesus. He gave His first and only Son because of His love for His family, for you and me and for all those who believe and put their trust in Him. He sent His only Son to earth because of His indescribable, extravagant, immeasurable love for us. Tears streamed down my face as I contemplated the depth of God's love.

Greater love has no one than this, than to
lay down one's life for his friends.
JOHN 15:13

With this revelation, I squeezed Jake even tighter and couldn't imagine him being beaten, ridiculed, humiliated, and dying for me to justify and pay for my sins. WOW! When I finally made it personal, it all began to make more sense and sink in. Think about it: It would be excruciating to watch your son go through it. But God loves unconditionally to the point of giving up His Son as the payment for the sin in the world. He forgives all of our sins through the sacrifice of His Son, Jesus. Someone had to pay for the sin, and Jesus willingly did it.

It is transforming when we understand the love of God and put our trust in Him. He did that for you and me because He loves us. Jesus loves you so much He died for YOU so you can be together for eternity in heaven and for an abundant life here on earth!

HONEY NUGGET

The God who created you loves you so fiercely that He gave His only Son so you could live with Him in freedom, forgiveness, and forever love.

CHAPTER 5

FIRST KISS

On an ordinary day in a very ordinary way, God showed me how much He loves using my sweet six-month-old baby, Jake. I was holding him on my hip in the kitchen. I had been kissing him, talking to him, and singing to him when he turned his head and launched in a super jerky movement at my face with an open mouth. He kissed me and continued to press his little head into mine. Our foreheads stayed connected while we enjoyed the close moment together. It was not a perfect kiss, but it was the first time he had shown affection toward me. My heart overflowed; his kiss was telling me he loved me too. I had loved him before I even found out I was pregnant and had wanted to have a baby for as long as I could remember. In a similar way, God loved us before we ever knew who God was too. He created and made us in His image and loved us extravagantly way before we ever knew Him, let alone loved Him, just as I did with Jake. Let that sink in a minute: God loved us before we even knew about Him. He created us, cared for us, provided for us, watched over us, and made plans for us before we ever heard of Him, let alone knew Him.

> *We love Him because He first loved us.*
> 1 JOHN 4:19

The security I got from that promise grounded me, making me feel love like I never had before. That is love. To love someone before you ever lay eyes on them is how I felt about my firstborn. It helped me understand God's character as well as I don't have to doubt His love for me or how much He has done for me and the great and mighty plans He has made. It was a shift in my perspective and outlook. So after I got the slobbery kiss on my jaw from Jake, my heart softened. What an incredible feeling to be loved by another. I didn't change the way I loved Jake; I loved him, period. What it did was transform my heart because of my view of God's love for me. Does God love me like I love Jake?

Yes.

Yes.

YES!!!

He loves perfectly and unconditionally. Did this build my confidence? Yes, so my understanding of God grew, and my trust in Him began to grow, too, little by little.

> *For I know the thoughts I think toward*
> *you, says the Lord, thoughts of peace and not*
> *of evil, to give you a future and a hope.*
> JEREMIAH 29:11

God used Jake to grow my faith. As I was looking and seeking, I found Him in the middle of the day with a sweet baby on my hip.

Where can you see God in your day? HE is right here with us, waiting for us to see Him. My hands-down favorite verse that I love comes after the famous verse I just quoted above and says the following:

> *And you will seek me and find me when*
> *you search for me with all your heart*
> **JEREMIAH 29:13**

I am on the lookout for God in all things. I want to see Him and know I can find Him because He says we can find Him in His Word. He isn't hiding, ready to scold us. He wants to love us. I want you to see Him in your life and feel His love like I felt Jake's love. He is so in love with you and waiting for you to see Him. Be like Jake. Lean in, give a big, wet kiss, and move toward Him. He is waiting for you.

HONEY NUGGET

God loved you long before you knew Him, and when you lean toward Him with even the smallest gesture of love, He's already there, embracing you with perfect, unshakable affection.

CHAPTER 6

WAY HIGHER, FAR BETTER

After Michael and I had our honeymoon baby, we were so elated with him that we decided to have another bundle of joy. Because we got pregnant with Jake so quickly, I never thought not getting pregnant would be an issue. I did not even think about it once. I am a planner and like everything in order, so "I planned" when we would get pregnant again so I could have a May baby. I don't know why, but May sounded like a good month. I wanted. I wanted. I wanted. While I was at it, I heard you could do some special things to determine the sex of the baby, so we did those "things" as well.

My mom friends shared that if you figure out when you ovulate, you go back so many days, which ensures a girl but the day you ovulate would be a boy. There was some notion that different positions would also elicit a boy or girl, not too sure how that works either but okay. (I don't know how scientific this is, so please don't try this at home based only on my recommendation.) I was in control mode, and it was not becoming of me as I was trying to control what the outcome would be. We had a son first, so how about a daughter this time? A baby girl, born in May, would be perfect.

August, the ideal month to get pregnant for a May baby, came and went, and I was shocked at getting my period. What? Not pregnant? Okay, next month. September would make Jake and the new baby's birthday the same month but two years apart. Perfect! That sounded organized and planned, but you would not believe it. To my shock, no baby. What in the world was happening? I was so obsessed with getting pregnant and trying to control the situation that I was probably unrecognizable to some. Sorry to all those who knew me then, especially my husband.

Looking back, I was so untrusting and showed zero faith in God with this matter. I was taking all the control and stress upon myself. I had not been praying to God about any of it. I just decided what I wanted and when, and then I tried to get it. When it didn't work, I had to pause and rethink my strategy. I must be a slow learner because this situation felt very similar to my husband searching, and if I had learned this simple strategy, I would not be stressed out and floundering. I needed to simply seek God and His plan for this second baby. I had been holding on tight to my way and not His way. But He says in His Word,

> For my thoughts are not your thoughts, neither are your
> ways my ways, declares the Lord. For as the heavens
> are higher than the earth, so are my ways higher than
> your ways and my thoughts than your thoughts.
>
> ISAIAH 55:8-9 ESV

After six months of trying to control when and what we were having as a second child, I was done. I finally did what I should have done from the start: place the control in God's hands. Why was I in my own little world and not asking God for help or direction? I knew this from two years ago when I let go of trying to control whom I would marry and God gave me Mr. More-Than-I-Could-Think-Or-Imagine, so I should do it again for this situation. It sounds so obvious, but it wasn't. I was living in a world where we were supposed to take control and be powerful and bold. It was not easy to submit and let go of my control. It was hard and uncomfortable, but it was also a relief. God knew what was best, and why in the world had I not done this sooner? God is so patient with me, and in this situation, He was gently guiding me to trust Him.

Before you hear the story's outcome and how God showed up, think about what you are holding onto tightly and not letting go of. What are you gripping and trying to plan without His direction? I love the saying about "eyes up." "Put your eyes up to Jesus." He is the answer. He is the way, the truth, and the life, no matter what you are going through—infertility, singleness, sickness, loneliness, heartbreak, etc.

> *But seek first the kingdom of God and His righteousness,*
> *and all these things shall be added to you.*
> MATTHEW 6:33

I love this verse so much; that word "seek" makes my heart flutter. He says, "Seek me first, and I will help you with it all." Well, in true God fashion, I got pregnant with our second baby in March, and the birth was in the exact month I was trying to avoid so that I wouldn't have a Christmas baby.

But God gifted us a baby in the perfect month that He knew was best.

> *God makes everything happen at the right time. Yet*
> *none of us can ever fully understand all he has done.*
> **ECCLESIASTES 3:11 CEV**

And God gave us the perfect baby BOY whom we named Luke and for whom we will forever be grateful.

> *For you formed my inward parts; You covered me*
> *in my mother's womb. I will praise You, for I am*
> *fearfully and wonderfully made; Marvelous are*
> *your works, and that my soul knows very well.*
> **PSALM 139:13-14**

I do not have enough words or the right words to explain whom the Lord gave us. From the moment they laid him on my chest, I knew Luke was exactly whom God had chosen for us and our family. He was a gift from the Lord and is a constant reminder that God knows, loves, and is patient and kind.

Luke was born on December 4, 2001, the month Jesus' birth is celebrated. Luke's birthdays have never been overlooked or diluted because of the busy month of December. You know what else? The Lord knew how much I would enjoy having a newborn three weeks before Christmas. It was a very special Christmas, where I snuggled and kissed Luke throughout the day, thanking the Lord for the BEST gift I could have ever received (besides Jesus) on Christmas.

I would never try to trade my ways for His ways, knowing whom (Luke) and when (December) He gave us. God is trustworthy. He is who He says He is, and He is active in my life. He does know what is best.

HONEY NUGGET

The moment we stop striving for control
we make room for God to do something
far greater than we imagined.

CHAPTER 7

FAMILY OVER FORTUNE

Michael spent nearly four years working alongside his father and stepmother, joining their established business as a co-owner to help expand and grow the company. The opportunities were limitless with this new partnership. When Michael joined them, they expanded their services from a general contracting business into a site development business where they worked with wireless operators in California. Michael was eager to build this company with the experience he had gained since college, and having lived in basically all four corners of the US and in Italy. Unfortunately, after a few years, the partnership started to decline. There was a lot of anger and bitterness, which was unhealthy and caused so much stress in everyone's life.

The three of them had different goals for the company: One wanted to grow and expand, and two wanted to stay status quo and enjoy life and the company's profits. That was detrimental not only to the company but also to their relationship with each other. There were huge disagreements, skipped holidays, and overall a spirit of heaviness in our relationship with them. We were asking God what to do and were praying with friends and advisors, and ultimately Michael felt like it was best to restore his relationship with his parents by leaving the company rather than staying and watching it deteriorate.

This was an extremely hard decision. On one hand, it might have seemed foolish to walk away when we could have stayed, endured, and collected the cash. But we felt the Lord was saying that restoration of the relationship was far more important and that He would provide what we needed to live. While Michael was on his way to pray with a friend prior to meeting with his father to discuss his departure, Michael sensed the Lord say, "Let go of this fish; I have a bigger fish for you." The company had grown by ten times since Michael had joined with lots of room to keep growing. My heart still races when I think about the events of the departure. It was hard and so scary as we were walking away from our income and livelihood. However, we trusted God that He had better plans for us, including the top priority of restoring our relationship with his parents. Sometimes it doesn't make sense, and it might look like the exact opposite thing we should do. But this was the verse that kept us secure during this season:

> *Trust the Lord with all your heart, and lean not*
> *on your own understanding; in all your ways*
> *acknowledge Him, and He shall direct your paths.*
> **PROVERBS 3:5-6**

Michael was being led by the Lord, and I was his admiring wife who followed and agreed, which was the easy part. I trusted my husband and his leading because I watched him seek the Lord and ask Him what he should do with this very difficult decision he had to make regarding his parents and the company. So it happened on that March day in 2002 that he left. We had a six-month severance and a whole lot of unknowns ahead of us, but we knew the Lord was in our corner.

HONEY NUGGET

Sometimes faith means walking away from comfort so you can walk closer to God's best for you.

THE CROSSROAD AND THE CROSS

What do you do when you walk away from the livelihood that once defined your security, only to find yourself at life's crossroads, uncertain which path will lead you forward? For Michael and me, we had no idea. But with God's help, we figured it out. It all started when Michael went on a guys' trip. His business mentor, Chris Crane, was also on the trip, and they had gone for an early morning run. Michael was telling him all the latest details about leaving the business he had with his father and stepmother. Chris stopped in his tracks, literally, put his arm on Michael's shoulder and said, "You and Heidi have to go do Crossroads Discipleship Training School (CDTS) at Youth with a Mission (YWAM) in Hawaii. It is life-changing, and you will get all the direction you need and more."

Youth with a Mission is a global, non-denominational Christian training and outreach organization founded by Loren and Darlene

Cunningham with the mission "to know God and make Him known." After completing a three-month training school, students are sent out into the world to share the hope of Jesus. Their ultimate goal is to make disciples of all nations, ensuring every person in every tribe has heard the Good News. It's a dynamic and impactful organization that continues to touch lives and transform communities around the world.

"Let's go to Hawaii to seek the Lord," Michael said the minute he walked in the door from his trip. Putting your life on hold for five months and flying to a tropical island to seek "direction" from God may sound crazy to some, and it certainly did to me too! How was I supposed to do this away from home with two babies (Jake was two and a half, and Luke was five months)? It sounded horrible and insane to me! But this whole book is to show you how the Lord speaks and shows up and what the Lord can do when you follow Him. This is when I started to seek Him for direction in making decisions, not just asking Him for "things" like husbands and babies. It was a new concept for me to know I could pray for direction and clarity for the path of my life.

As great as YWAM sounded, I was adamant about NOT going to Hawaii to do our Crossroads Discipleship Training School. I changed the subject when Michael brought it up and continued to ignore it as an option for us. There was just no way I was packing up two little babies and all their stuff and leaving with them for five months.

One day the tension finally broke, and we made a plan. One of Michael's friends stopped by the house to say hello. He was standing at the front door, casually chatting with us, when he looked at me and said, "So I hear you are going to Youth with a Mission to do your Crossroads Discipleship Training School in May. That is so exciting." I was in absolute disbelief. My head was spinning, and I was sure my eyes crossed. "No, sir, I don't know what you are talking about! Not us!" I wanted to say, but I tried to act politely and smiled instead. I looked at Michael and thought a lot of things in my head that I wanted to say that were not nice or honoring of him.

Michael and I were NOT on the same page at this point in our journey. He told people we were going, and I wasn't even considering it. We were so young and did not act as "one" in marriage when making this decision, both living like singles and not united. After this guy dropped the atomic bomb on my life and left, we finally, calmly (very surprisingly), discussed YWAM together. I was able to tell him how adamant I was about not going. "No, I don't want to go. No, it will be too hard; I can't do this with the boys; I don't want to leave my family. No! No! No! No!" I was so sad and distraught, not wanting to follow my husband's lead. Sure, you can leave your prior business but don't make me move with these little babies to a one room dorm situation for three months and then to God knows where in the world for two more months on outreach. Life was hard enough here in the comfort of our normal surroundings of home.

So Michael said gently, "Let's ask God what we should do, and if He can open all the doors and help us complete the list of items we have to do in order to go, then we will have our answer." I agreed but thought there was no way we could get all this done in three short weeks before the next class would start in May 2002.

The biggest door that needed opening was securing a nanny to care for the boys during the day when I would be in class from 8 a.m. to 3 p.m. Monday through Friday. I asked all my younger siblings if anyone would want to go to Hawaii for three months and help us. Understandably, they all had jobs and plans and were unable to go. I asked our amazing babysitters (Amanda and Melissa), friends' babysitters, teen neighbors, and everyone we thought would fit the job, but not one could go. YES! I was happy to NOT find a nanny to go with us!

But Michael decided to call YWAM's office and inquire about employing a nanny already living there. If you don't know Michael, he is very persistent and will think outside of the box to get to the end goal. I had seen him do this countless times, so I should have known he would be tackling this hindrance head on. Sadly (but not sadly), the nanny we were put in contact with sounded amazing but was already hired. Katie was seventeen years old and lived in Hawaii with her parents, who served on the YWAM staff, along with her younger fourteen-year-old sister, Shelly. Unfortunately, another family had already secured her as a nanny for them while they came from Europe to do their CDTS (Crossroads Discipleship Training School). And there was another family on the waiting list for her so that made us third on the list. We were so close but still, it was a no.

We continued to look for a nanny to take with us but found no one. Michael continued to work on the checklist of other items that needed to be done. The class start date was now only two weeks away. I thought for sure we were staying home, and I was so relieved. But this would be a very boring story if I told you we never went.

Guess how God showed up and opened our final door to go? Unexpectedly, Katie called Michael and said, "You won't believe this, but both families had to cancel and are not coming, so I am available to nanny for your two boys." Not only did we land the jackpot of all nannies, but everything else fell perfectly into place. We had the funds secured, a house sitter lined up for our San Diego home, points ready to cover our plane tickets, applications submitted, and Luke cleared for travel after his earlier RSV hospitalization at just four months old, the very day Michael had left his previous company.

Everything we asked the Lord for was taken care of within those three weeks. It was out of my control, for we were on our way for the adventure of a lifetime to do our Crossroads Discipleship Training School in Kona, Hawaii.

Michael was elated. I, on the other hand, was extremely skeptical and still hesitant, questioning how all this happened. I thought it was just by chance all the items were taken care of. Or were they? Was it Michael's persistence, great timing, and perfect circumstances that made it all happen?

Looking back after it all happened and now knowing who God is, I know these were God's beautiful drops of goodness and honey in our life. The hurdles we had to jump in such a short time frame were impossible without God's help. Although I questioned Him and how this all came together at the time, God had always been constant and capable.

Our time at YWAM was the most incredible time of my life and forever changed and transformed me. I have thanked Michael a thousand times over for "dragging" me there because I would have missed out on the most transformative time of my life. I understood God like I never had before because "it is only in God that we discover our origin, our identity, our meaning, our purpose, our significance, and our destiny. Every other path leads to a dead end."[1]

HONEY NUGGET

When every need is placed in His hands, God weaves the impossible into a testimony of His faithfulness.

CHAPTER 9

COCKROACHES AND FINDING JESUS

We lived on the Youth with a Mission (YWAM) base for three months in Kona, Hawaii, in a studio that was about the size of my bathroom in San Diego. That was not a typo; it is supposed to say bathroom, not bedroom. Yes, our little family of four lived in one tiny studio where at first I thought I might die.

Seriously. We had a toddler bed for Jake, who was two and a half, a pack-and-play for five-month-old Luke, two twin beds shoved together that were about five inches different in height for Michael and me, a small wicker loveseat, and a refrigerator that was dually used as an AC unit. When we were desperate to cool off the room, we would open the refrigerator door and put a fan in front of it. Don't tell my dad as he would have a heart attack knowing this. But when it was humid and sooo hot with no air flow, those desperate times called for desperate measures.

Little did we know our quaint little room was already occupied by uninvited guests, a scorpion comfortably nestled under Luke's pack-and-play and countless families of cockroaches and geckos. Each morning I would awaken to geckos crawling on the ceiling right above my head. The urge to let out a piercing scream was almost irresistible. I found myself in a constant state of shock, jumping, screeching, and gasping at these little creatures all over our room. During the night, I would get up to feed Luke, turn on a little nightlight, and the dim light would reveal five-inch roaches coming to life and scurrying around the room. Eeek!

Side note for your knowledge (but mostly for your entertainment): Creatures and I don't mix. I don't like any insects, camping, or being dirty. One time I vividly recall almost hyperventilating when a colossal spider, the size of a coffee cup, crawled toward my face as I reached for a bunch of white towels to wash off the floor. I called my husband at work on the phone for help because in my world this was an emergency. I kept repeating, "There's a spider in the house; there's a spider in the house!" But all he heard was, "There is a fire in the house! There is a fire in the house!" To this day, before I wrap my white towel around my body to dry off after a shower, I check for spiders. I am most uncomfortable with any and all insects and creepy creatures. You must be wondering how I ever chose to allow bees on the front cover of this book. It was a tough decision for me, but I did it for the theme.

Another beautiful feature our room had was that one of the four walls was wide open, allowing air, sound, and light (and unwanted guests) to come in. There was no door or drape, just a screen wall so the entire building could hear every time my two year old yelled or my five month old cried. We had no TV, and this was back before mobile phones. How did we do it? Bob Goff says it so well, "Following Jesus means climbing, tripping, dusting ourselves off, and climbing some more. Faith isn't a business trip walked on a sidewalk; it's an adventure worked out on a steep and sometimes difficult trail."[2] That is how we did it. We were on the adventure of a lifetime! This metaphor of faith as a rugged journey illustrates that profound transformation happens when we step into challenges, not when we stick with the familiar. But in the end, the trip was worth every creepy crawly moment, and we would do it all again in a second.

When we first moved in, I would have done anything to have a different room. But after three heart-changing months, I wouldn't trade living in that "wild animal kingdom" room for anything. God allowed us to have the worst room, in my humble opinion, on the campus for a reason. You see, we left a beautiful house in San Diego and had every amenity we ever needed. Why would I choose this room again? Because this room was the learning ground that I needed to grow. The boys did not care where they lived as they just wanted to be cared for and with us. I needed the struggle to see if I could survive with geckos and no air conditioning. Thankfully, I saw the Lord provide the sweetest environment for our family. It was so amazing to spend time with my husband who previously worked sixteen-hour-plus days. We had the best talks and discussions and really reconnected during those months. We had each other and the Lord and found out that was all that was important. We didn't need all the fluff of stuff, just the bare necessities to live, and we enjoyed it. We recalibrated our life and discovered what was important in that little, cockroach-infested room.

I began to really understand the heart of God and His love for me and the world during our Crossroads Discipleship Training School.

During those three months, Monday through Friday, we went to "class" and heard from various speakers from around the world. Every week there were new subjects like the Father heart of God, forgiveness, prayer, spiritual warfare, discipleship, etc. I started to understand how faithful God was and started to look outside my tiny view of what I saw and began to see time, history, and the relevance of the Lord in an all-new way. I started to look through the lens of what God saw, taking off my lens and putting on His. It was mind-blowing. Remember I said how skeptical I was to even go on this adventure? Well, it took me about three weeks to finally let go, dig into what I was learning, and be open to really seeking the Lord for the first time. I wrote in my journal, took notes during class, sang the most amazing worship songs to live music every morning, read my Bible for the first time, and really started to see the brilliance of it all. Once I had a little taste of His goodness, I couldn't get enough. I had so many questions as I couldn't read or hear enough about the Lord. What happened to my heart? What happened was I fell in love with the

KING OF KINGS AND LORD OF LORDS!

REVELATION 19:16

I fell head over heels for the King, Creator, Sustainer of the Universe, who became the new King of my heart. This experience changed my life forever.

> *And do not be conformed to this world, but be transformed*
> *by the renewing of your mind, that you may prove what*
> *is that good and acceptable and perfect will of God.*

ROMANS 12:2

I came to understand God in a profound way, realizing that He loved me before I ever knew of Him. He gave me life, my family, and every good and perfect gift I cherished. He gave up His only begotten Son so I could have eternal life. His forgiveness washed away all the stupid and reckless things I had done. I had a renewed sense of purpose and a noticeable pep in my step as I was forgiven and given a fresh start.

I surrendered my life to God, allowing Him to take the helm as the Manager of my life and the King sitting on the throne; in doing so, I released my desires for control and perfection. While I admit that I sometimes find myself attempting to reclaim the throne, I make a conscious effort to get off the throne and surrender it back to Him each day. I said in my heart, "I believe You, and I will trust that You know what is best." By surrendering, I no longer had the pressure to do everything perfectly.

Being human is hard, but surrendering has also provided me with a comforting sense of direction, knowing that I have Someone who knows and understands me better than I know myself. It was so freeing and so exciting. He created me, so, of course, He knows every detail of who I am. I had Someone who loved me unconditionally, just as I have always longed to be loved.

> *Everyone who hears my words and obeys them is*
> *like a wise man who built his house on rock.*
> MATTHEW 7:24 NCV

And so I have to ask you the most important questions of your life:

Have you surrendered your life completely to God by placing your trust in God the Father, who willingly sent

His Son, Jesus, to earth so that you could receive full for-giveness for your mistakes and wrongdoings? Have you invited Jesus to be the Ruler of your life, rather than striving in your own strength?

This is the single most important, life-changing decision you will ever make, the firm foundation you can stand on and trust with every part of your life. When you choose to put your trust in Him and surrender the throne of your life to Him, everything changes. He becomes your steady Rock, your good Father, your loving Comforter, and the gentle Guide for every step you take. If you have never prayed this before or if you want to renew your heart and surrender again—I invite you to pray this prayer today:

> Dear Jesus,
>
> You have promised that if I believe in You, all my sins will be forgiven and You will welcome me, both now and for eternity in heaven. I confess my sins to You and ask for Your forgiveness. Please receive me into Your family as my Lord and Savior. I trust Your Word that salvation comes by grace through faith, not by anything I can do. Today, I surrender every part of my life to You, making You the Lord, Leader, and King of my heart. Thank You for loving me unconditionally. I commit my life fully to You.
>
> In Jesus' name, Amen.

I am praying for you, and I have been praying for this moment for you.

If you prayed that prayer, you are now in God's family forever! You have crossed the line by making the best decision of your entire life.

> *Therefore, if anyone is in Christ, he is a*
> *new creation, old things have passed away;*
> *behold, all things have become new.*
> 2 CORINTHIANS 5:17

Open your Bible and find that verse and in the margin write the date and "This is the day I gave my heart to the Lord!" Here is where the beautiful journey begins. Your life is going to be more abundant and full and have a new purpose. You will have the confidence to know and trust and follow and seek the Lord.

> *I have come that they may have life, and that*
> *they may have it more abundantly*
> JOHN 10:10

Your life will never be the same as you learn more about God and get to know Him more. It is not about religion but rather a relationship with Him. There are so many promises in the Word of God for you. Your life is now nestled firmly on the rock solid foundation of the Lord. It is an immovable rock of salvation and foundation for you to live your life from.

> *But you are a chosen generation, a royal priesthood,*
> *a holy nation, His own special people, that you may*
> *proclaim the praises of Him who called you out of*
> *darkness into His marvelous light; who once were*

not a people but are now the people of God, who had
not obtained mercy but now have obtained mercy.
1 PETER 2:9-10

You also have a new identity: You are God's precious child, and nothing can ever take that away from you or from me. That is the unshakable truth. Every other identity we hold, whether it is a role, title, or label, can change in an instant. And if our sense of self is built on something that can be taken away, our world will crumble when it does. That's why God calls us to root our identity in Him alone. He is unchanging, immovable, and forever constant. I'll share more about this in the "Yellow Butterflies" story, but for now, hold tightly to this: Your identity in Christ is the only one that will never fade or fail.

What you hopefully have done just now in the quiet of your heart or with a trusted friend is what I did in Kona. This is where I crossed the line and really, really surrendered my heart to Jesus forever. I knew of Him and saw glimpses of Him, but this was different. I was making the decision to accept this free gift of salvation and believe Him wholeheartedly one hundred percent.

My heart was overflowing with excitement with this new decision. I had so many questions and couldn't wait to go to "class" and hear the speakers now that I understood and believed in not only God and His sovereignty but also that the Bible was His living Word. It was all true and an instruction Book for me to read about life. It was all there.

I talked to one of Michael's best friends, Barry, who had been a Christian for a long time, on the phone and asked him many questions I believe we all have about God: Where did God come from?

How is this Bible alive and relevant? How does God speak to us? How do we hear from Him? How do we know He is real? How much does God love us? Two of the verses he shared that helped me wrap my brain around where to start were John 1:1-2:

> *In the beginning was the Word, and the*
> *Word was with God, and the Word was*
> *God. He was in the beginning with God.*

That truth blew me away. Wow! I was just walking into this amazing truth that God has been around from the very beginning and He planned everything, including me too. It is a lot to digest when you look from God's perspective and how much He is involved in our life. This was the first date and note I had ever written in my new Bible, writing in the margin of that verse so I could remember and look back at my faith journey. It was July 1, 2002. I was so excited to learn and felt like I was drinking from a fire hose. I couldn't get enough of Him. I learned so much about God and myself during that summer. It changed everything about my life in all the best ways.

For our homework in school, we kept a journal that had specific components to it. We had to write three parts in our journal: First, a short summary of the week, second, what we learned that week, and third, how we were going to apply it or make a change to our lives. It activated my growth, and I was thriving.

So you know how I said I was a baby Christian? Well, I was so new in my faith that I had never prayed out loud before. I was thirty-one years old and had only prayed a little bit in my head or memorized prayers in a group setting. So on week three of being in Kona, I felt very compelled to have my application for the week be to pray with

Michael out loud. He was my husband for heaven's sake, and we did a lot of other things together, so why wouldn't we pray together? Do you know why I hadn't prayed with him before? Because I was scared, fearful of what I would say and how it would sound and if it would be good enough. What does God say about that statement I just made?

> *There is no fear in love; but perfect love casts*
> *out fear, because fear involves torment. But he*
> *who fears has not been made perfect in love.*
> 1 JOHN 4:18

As I write this now, I am saddened for myself. What a trap! I wasn't praying with my husband because I was afraid of not doing it right. Well, I broke that fear by doing it. That night, we laid in bed facing each other and holding hands, and I said, "Can I pray too?" I am sure if Michael wasn't lying down, he may have fainted! He had never heard me pray, and we had been married for almost four years at that point. I prayed, and it felt so good. I didn't have to rely on myself to say it right. The Holy Spirit was with me and directing my words of what to pray. What a freeing experience that changed my entire life. Do you know how much I LOVE PRAYING NOW? It is so ironic because it is one of my favorite things to do. The very thing that I was fearful of doing before.

So, now it is your turn: What are you afraid of? What is holding you back? Is there something you know you should do but you have been stonewalling? I am here to encourage you, dear friend, to make a plan and do it. Instead of saying you can't do it, try it and step out in faith. I believe you can do it, and I believe the Lord is gentle and guiding your every step.

It is pure joy to be in fellowship and in communion with the Lord of the universe. Praying built my faith and helped my relationship with the Lord grow. Not that He is a magical genie who grants wishes, but He is a loving Father who knows the absolute best and will answer with a yes, no, or not yet. I love this about Him so much that I don't need to hold onto the stress and the burden of life but rather:

> *Be anxious for nothing , but in everything by prayer*
> *and supplication, with thanksgiving, let your*
> *requests be made known to God; and the peace of*
> *God, which surpasses all understanding, will guard*
> *your hearts and minds through Christ Jesus.*
>
> PHILIPPIANS 4:6-7

HONEY NUGGET

God often uses the most unexpected and challenging seasons to draw us closer to Him and reveal the depth of His love.

CHAPTER 10

OUTREACH ANYONE?

After three months of learning about God's amazing and extravagant heart for us at the University of the Nations in Kona, our Crossroads Discipleship Training School class of forty people was going on an outreach/mission trip to the Philippines for two months. Remember me? I was in the same place again, wondering how in the world I was to do this with a now three year old and an eight month old. Instead of trying to figure it out on our own, we immediately asked God for direction.

Those three months taught me to seek the Lord first. It sure looked like we were supposed to go; it looked so right. A mission trip? How could you say no to Jesus, to helping people know Jesus, or to serving people in Jesus' name? You have been trained to go out and serve others, so why wouldn't you go? But we had ZERO peace about going. Every time we talked about it I felt anxious and uneasy. The poor guy in charge of the outreach had talked to us so many times. He needed to know if we were going, and rightly so, as he was planning a huge trip for forty people to fly halfway across the world and help the needy. There was a lot to do. Every time he saw us he asked if we were going. It got to a point I thought I might have something wrong with me because when I saw him coming, I would freeze up and freak out and walk the other way.

After all, we still didn't know if we were going. It was consuming us, but thankfully, Michael felt the exact same way I did. We prayed and asked God to give us peace about going. We had everything else lined up to go: the funds, the time, the training, absolutely everything. We just didn't have the peace. Something felt off and wrong. We asked other classmates to pray for us, but no one had heard that we were to go either. So we had still not decided, and the final deadline for purchasing tickets was upon us. We just couldn't say yes confidently.

Then God stepped in and made the way clear. It just so happened on that long-awaited Saturday, we decided to splurge and treat ourselves to some good ol' McDonald's for lunch. Michael prayed a very simple prayer over our burgers and fries, saying, "I guess we are not to go, Lord, because we don't have any peace and thanks for this decadent meal." A few hours later, when I was outside with Jake playing at the park, I realized I had the peace I longed for. I was not toiling and anxious but felt light as a feather. I didn't have a million things racing through my mind. I felt like the Lord had spoken and confirmed our not going. Michael also expressed a peace came over him after we confirmed the Lord was telling us not to go. I love this so much because I learned a valuable lesson. It might look right, holy, and good, but if we ask Him, the Lord knows what we are to do and will tell us even when we think we already know the answer. I need to ask Him about everything.

It makes me think about the many choices we face in life. God has given us the extravagant gift of free will. It is a beautiful but sometimes daunting responsibility, especially for someone like me, the self-proclaimed Queen of the Land of Indecision. At times I don't want to choose, or I'm unsure which way to go. But God didn't make us robots or puppets; He created us with capable minds, rich experiences, supportive relationships, emotions, His Word, and the greatest Helper of all—the Holy Spirit. We can make good decisions, and I don't need to fret.

Knowing I can turn to the all-knowing King of the universe for counsel changes everything. He knows me, He knows what's ahead, and He knows the outcome. That truth relieves the pressure of trying to figure life out on my own. The most important question becomes simple: What does God say?

Nor do we know what to do, but our eyes are upon You.
2 Chronicles 20:12

For those who love what you reveal, everything fits—
no stumbling around in the dark for them. I wait
expectantly for your salvation; God, I do what you tell
me. My soul guards and keeps all your instructions—oh
how much I love them! I follow your directions, abide
by your counsel; my life's an open book before you.
Psalm 119:165-168 msg

Months later in San Diego, we had further confirmation that we had heard correctly from the Lord not to go when our friends and

classmates who went to the Philippines told us that it was a difficult trip, full of hardships. They said it would have been even harder
with Jake and Luke there since they were so young. Thank You, Lord!
You knew.

What are you thinking about in your life right now? Is there a decision looming that you are availing or toiling over? I want to encourage you to open your hands and ask God to help you and show you
the next steps. Set everything down, open your palms, and give it to
Him. The best and most exciting part is that if you have asked Him,
He will answer you. Some of you may think I am nuts but hold on.
If you have read this far into the book, then I believe you are still
curious and have some idea of who God is. I promise you I am not
crazy. God is waiting for you. Ask Him your question. Give Him
your prayer.

> *And you will seek Me and find Me, when*
> *you search for Me with all your heart.*
> **JEREMIAH 29:13**

HONEY NUGGET

*When you place every decision in God's
hands, He will guide you to do what is
best, not just what seems good, by replacing
uncertainty with clarity and peace.*

CHAPTER 11

MOMMA BEAR

After our three glorious months in Kona, Hawaii, at the YWAM base, we returned to San Diego. We were filled to the brim with God's Word and gained so much knowledge and truth that we were ready to take on the world. We had a whole new perspective on life, and God empowered us to do great and mighty things for Him. We had a new purpose in life. What wasn't filled up was our bank account as it was dwindling, and the stress of life was at its peak.

One month after we returned home to San Diego, we found out we were having our third baby! We were elated, of course, but let me restate what was happening in our lives. It was a lot.

- Starting a new company from our extra bedroom
- No income, bank account dwindling
- Three year old
- Nine month old
- Pregnant

I have a hard time remembering all the day-to-day details because I was exhausted and sick. Jake and Luke were busy little boys who took all of my attention. I did the best I could with my limited energy and sickness from the new pregnancy. But something had shifted in my heart since I understood who God was. My life goals and purpose had changed. I understood my new role as a JESUS-LOVING MOM. I couldn't do enough to point my two little boys to the goodness of God. So to my sheer delight I found the Scripture that says,

> *I have no greater joy than to hear*
> *that my children walk in truth.*
>
> 3 JOHN 4

That was my new life verse for being a mom. I wanted to do everything I was asked to do to point my boys to Jesus so they could walk in the truth. This world is hard and can be cruel, and the only way is to do it with Jesus.

> *These things I have spoken to you, that in Me you may*
> *have peace. In the world you will have tribulation;*
> *but be of good cheer, I have overcome the world.*
>
> JOHN 16:33

I couldn't force our boys into anything, just like God didn't force me. It was my choice, and it was their choice. But I made it my new mission and purpose to point them to Him, and someday, they would hopefully choose to believe, follow, and trust Him on their own. Getting that new purpose in my motherhood changed so much for me (and them). Have you heard the analogy about a pilot navigating to a destination, and by miscalculating by one degree, the plane would land in the wrong location? For every mile the plane traveled, it would be off by ninety-two feet. That may not seem like a big deal as you fly over the Atlantic from New York toward Paris because you will still land in Europe. But if you travel from California to Honolulu, the destination would be forty miles away from the island. You would land in the middle of the Pacific Ocean.

I love this comparison to parenting. Where are we headed, and what is the goal of parenting? There is so much to do for them, but where are you headed? I am forever grateful that I could see the importance of this simple illustration and make our destination and goal of parenting to always point our children to JESUS. He is the landing destination that I am on for my children; that was the most important thing I could do as a mom to them. The change in my heart and the purpose of my parenting had been shifted, even if it was only one degree. Yet it changed everything about our children's futures.

God had entrusted me with these little boys to raise them and fill them up to the fullest with truth and love. I was so excited to take on this new role and do it to the best of my ability. Not that I wasn't doing that before, but I wasn't doing it with the same end goal. I had to change my destination point and intentionally steer the plane toward it, even if it took eighteen to twenty years to land the plane. It was overwhelming when I looked at the end goal, but all I needed to do was be intentional. Point those boys to truth and what the Word said, not culture, the latest fad, or the world, and be deliberate about what went on in my boys' lives.

How did God encourage me and give me a new destination to aim for? What did God say about me being their mom? He said in so many words to me (and to you moms out there):

I picked YOU to be their mom, not anyone else. This job is for you. Take this job seriously. Love is not enough. Being a good nurturer is not enough. Show, model, and point those boys to Me. And for all your family, friends, and neighbors whom I put in your path, show them who I am too. It is not just being nice and kind to all. Be picky, be smart, and make wise choices. Ask Me what to do and how to do it. I will help you and guide you. I know these kids and every little detail about them. I have mighty plans for these children; they need to know Me, and I have hand-picked you to do it. Get on it! Don't waste another day!

Do not take this the wrong way if you have a nanny, but I let go of the nanny I had in San Diego. I had her for all the wrong reasons because all my friends and neighbors had nannies. I had one solely because I was going with the crowd and following culture. It sounded cool, "I have a nanny!" For what? So I could go to the store, the gym, and drive around alone? For me and my specific circumstances, I was led to leave my first-grade teaching job that I LOVED to stay home and be the primary caregiver to my kids. So why did I have a nanny? Was she necessary? No, I didn't have her so I could work. I had her so I could play. I am so thankful the Lord gently showed me that there was a better way for our family.

Being in Kona, digging into the Word of God, and aligning my priorities with God's priorities made my life come into focus. I had a new, unshakable identity that no one could take away from me. I was God's daughter and hand-picked to be my boys' mom. I concluded that I needed a cleaning lady and weekly babysitter to get out of the house for appointments and date nights.

I found time daily to open my Bible and seek the Lord, even if it was only for ten minutes, even if I had a baby on my lap. I opened my Bible every day to hear from God. It was His love letter to me. It is His love letter to you. What Scripture did He want me to read? What did He want to say to me?

I also read many Christian parenting books because I was determined to be the mom I was called to be! Some of the most impactful books that shaped my parenting to reflect Jesus' heart were *Parenting by the Book* and *Teen-Proofing* by John Rosemond. I would say they were the most helpful books I read. I understood why I needed to teach my children to respect authority and be obedient the first time I asked. Rosemond helped me understand the importance of both because these littles needed to respect and obey me and they needed to do the same for Him. This simple discipline of listening and obeying would carry over into their lives the rest of their lives. The parenting tools and explanations had a long-term reason and effect that proved to be of the utmost importance. As I said, that book solidified and grounded me as a parent.

I am getting ahead of myself in explaining this because I only have two of the three children at this point in the story. Still, I must tell you now: For those of you with teenagers or approaching teens, the most impactful book I read besides the Bible was *Teen-Proofing* by John Rosemond. It was incredible when the boys were becoming so much more independent from us. They needed to know how to manage their money, manage their time, deal with friends, drugs, etc. We only had a few short years left before they would be on their own, so we had to prepare them and know that they could care for themselves and thrive. The list of what they needed to do and do well was long. But with God, His strength and direction, and the guidance of these books, we did it.

*I will instruct you and teach you in the way you
should go; I will guide you with My eye.*
PSALM 32:8

Another powerful shift in me was my attitude toward my husband and children. There is a very seductive yet destructive moment in culture right now toward motherhood and wifehood. The funny jokes that dismiss our husbands and the exasperating stories about how burdensome our children are to us as wives and mothers are numerous. My heart shrieks inside when I hear moms say how excited they are for summer to end so they can get the kids out of the house. Or moms gone wild at moms' night out when they get away from their husbands and children. Ouch! And even worse, these poor children who hear their moms say it about them; that saddens my heart so much. I am not saying I have this figured out perfectly at all, but I made a point not to ever say anything about whether I couldn't wait to send my kids to camp or get them to school or get rid of them, whether I said it in front of them or not. I am not saying to keep them home and grin and bear it either; kids need to do all kinds of things to grow, with and without us. I am also not saying it is easy to have kids at home and be the cook, entertainer, driver, housemaid, laundry service, and all the other endless things moms are entrusted to do. It is hard work, harder than teaching twenty-seven kindergarteners. Let me tell you; I have done both. The point I am trying to share is that the shift in my heart and mind when I spoke of them was imperative. It is not funny to "joke" about how happy you will be when they are gone.

This short time of motherhood when our kids are home and demand so much of us is a season that will pass and be gone before we know it. We have all heard and/or experienced "the days are long, but the years are short." We should receive each day as a gift with these kids and do our very best by embracing this season of mother-hood to the best of our ability. For such a time as this we have been given this amazing responsibility.

> *To everything there is a season, a time*
> *for every purpose under heaven.*
> Ecclesiastes 3:1

I have a story to show you an example of my new renewed atti-tude and purpose. It broke my heart when I was at the mall with Jake and Luke in a double stroller. I was just showing the little bump of my third baby. We had two boys, so everyone, I mean everyone, was curious about the gender of baby number three. When she saw my bump, a lady approached me and asked what I was having. I told her we were waiting to have a surprise. She continued saying how she wished I would have a girl because boys are so hard and physical. "Girls are so much better, and you poor thing, I really hope it is a girl." *Ummm, excuse me, my boys can hear you*, I thought as I looked down at them in the stroller. Their big eyes looked at me with a hint of desperation. I remember turning into Momma Bear when I encoun-tered these interactions because this was not the first time. I explained how much I loved having boys and would be absolutely delighted to have another boy. God knows and has a plan! I was trying to be kind and pleasant, but I really wanted to tell her to stop and walk away (because I had a few other choice words that were not very nice).

Can I tell you what my boys' faces looked like? They watched me and heard me celebrate who they were, how much I enjoyed them, and my absolute love for them. Their little faces relaxed as they watched me debunk this destructive bullet and defuse the untruth bomb. I never wanted them to question who they were and who God made them to be. They are masterpieces! Never in a million years would I ever want them to think they were not exactly whom we wanted or God had made! I became an expert at this because even after our third little bundle was born, all kinds of unkind words were shot at us. Momma Bear is who I became in defending God's plan and, even more so, His creation.

HONEY NUGGET

God has hand-picked you for the sacred role you hold, and when you parent with His purpose in mind, every small, intentional choice can shape a child's life toward the truth that will anchor them forever.

CHAPTER 12

MD7

My purpose and goals had changed for my life after surrendering my life to the Lord. Michael had also changed as he was on fire for the Lord and the purpose of this new company he wanted to start. Leaving his parents' company was difficult, but the Lord was with him and guided him to start another company on his own. Like everything, it started small: one-man-strong small. He worked in our extra upstairs bedroom. He wanted to expand the business idea of his last company to manage all of the assets of the wireless companies in the US. He wanted to build a company with God at the helm, leading, directing, and paving the way. This was not his or our company; it was the Lord's company. Everything about it was His.

For Michael, life after YWAM meant putting God, his family, and us first, and then work. The sweetness of that statement is like a double-filled chocolate lava cake with decadent gelato on the side or a freshly baked chocolate chip cookie with my morning coffee. It was so sweet to have a husband seek the Lord in all his things, including us. Work was always an understandable priority since he was the main provider for the boys and me. It wasn't like he didn't have that priority, but he reprioritized it. The change in him was night and day. He limited his work hours to being home for dinner and time with the boys now. He still worked his tail off, but he worked smarter.

Michael knew he didn't want to be on the mission field after YWAM, but he had a clear picture of starting a business and making God the center of it all. He read the book *Anointed for Business* by Ed Silvoso, and he was off to the races. He was so encouraged about building this company with God that he bought a trunk full of those books and handed them out to pretty much everyone he met, including strangers at Starbucks.

As you can imagine, our home was a bit chaotic with the young boys: Jake was three years old, Luke was nine months old, and Michael was working from home. If you know, you know. It was crazy and exhausting, but we put our faith in Jesus that we were not alone and that He would lead us every day. Michael had left his job and company and needed to know how to provide for us. We had a severance that would hold us for over six months, and it expired quickly.

After a few weeks of Michael working from the "office" upstairs in our house, he moved offices. It was really difficult for him (and me) to have small little ones in the house. So he instead found 2,500 new offices around our town and the country that were for the most part quiet and served a great cup of coffee. He made the popular coffee shop his new daily office. It was much more manageable, and we were both relieved. I didn't have to stress about the boys being loud while he was on the phone or him waking the boys with his voice carrying through the walls of the bedrooms. From August 2002 until January 2003, he worked very hard to make a business plan and confirm this new budding plan was on the right track. He named the company MD7. A good friend helped him come up with the name which was so clever in my opinion. M is for Michael, D is for David, and 7 is the seventh letter in the alphabet for Gianni. By divine appointments, blood, sweat, tears, and prayers, Michael's vision was becoming real and happening.

So, what do you think?
With God on our side like this, how can we lose?
ROMANS 8:31 MSG

In the early months of MD7, two dear friends began a prayer group with Michael. Since November 2002 this group has been praying for all the employees, their families and the company's success. If you work at MD7 or know someone who has, I guarantee they have been prayed for by Michael and these faithful friends. The prayers that have been said on those Tuesday mornings are infinite. God has done miraculous work using this company, but that will be another book, I am sure of it. The Tuesday morning prayer meeting still exists and is going strong after twenty-three years and counting.

In those early days Michael was eagerly seeking a contract from the wireless carriers to help them manage their wireless portfolios. His dream was to help these mobile phone operators manage, develop, and optimize their networks by doing all the back-of-the-office work so they could focus on their core job of expanding and upgrading the network. Day after day, he got closer and closer. Over the first few months, more divine appointments came to MD7, and he worked for the company with no pay. However, it was a beautiful time to trust and see God answer so many prayers.

As I mentioned, our bank account was shrinking, and we had no income. We lived very carefully not to spend more than we had as we did not want to go into debt because of the start-up. But the day we dreaded finally came: the coffers were empty. Yet we knew God was faithful and trustworthy, so we took on every day as though the battle was already won. We trusted Him with it all but knew we had to do something. After we borrowed money from my dad and did not want to go into debt any further, we decided to put our house up for sale. After praying over it for weeks, we just could not afford it any longer. We were sad about selling it, but we had to do it. Having used every resource possible to keep it, we had to let go. My husband's stress over the mortgage was not worth us keeping the house.

We had bought this house when Jake was ten months old, and we were excited to have our family live there forever. We loved our home, which had rooms for our three children that we hoped to have someday. Being pregnant this third time was so bittersweet; the final empty room had been chosen for this little baby that was due in June, but it wasn't meant to be. It was also the first time in my life that I used a debit card at the grocery store and prayed that it would go through. We know what it is like to live on close to nothing, pray, and see God help us repeatedly. But we were a hundred percent sure the house had to go. We felt it was the right thing to do then and that God would lead us to the next place.

My dad was a successful real estate broker, so we asked him to help us sell the house we loved. A few days later, he came up and took pictures of the house. We both felt good about selling it and knew God had a plan for our growing family. This was just a house, and we could live anywhere if we had made it through living in the "wild animal kingdom" room in Kona. We walked my dad to the driveway and continued talking about listing the house the next day. Just then, Michael's mobile phone rang in his pocket. He walked away from us and up the street on what seemed like an important phone call. Are you ready to hear what God did?

Michael landed his first contract, and it was going to help us! Michael returned with a smile on his face and said, "Hank, we are keeping the house! We are starting work on our first contract!" The relief on his face, and frankly my dad's, was night and day compared to just moments prior. God had a plan, even though He took us down to the wire to reveal it to us. Michael had been building MD7 for thirteen months, and at the very moment that we were officially surrendering our home, the phone rang. God was so good at taking care of us as there was no need to sell the house because we knew the company would get off the ground.

It reminds me of the story of when God asked Abraham to sacrifice his own son Isaac, the same son that he was promised by God (Genesis 22:1-2). Abraham took one step in front of the other in obedience to the Lord. Did he want to kill his son whom he had prayed for and waited for with his wife Sarah for eighty years? No. Did we want to sell our first dream home that we bought together to raise our growing family? No. But we were willing to. We were putting the house on the market. And just like Abraham heard to stop the sacrifice as he raised his knife up in the air about to sacrifice Isaac, we were told we didn't need to list our house on the market and sell it. God was testing Abraham, and I believe God also tested us. Would we give up our home for Him? Would we trust Him with our family and future? Would we trust God to provide what we need to live and do what He asks (Genesis 22:8)?

Even though we knew work was coming, we still had no money

in the bank. We still had the mortgage and the normal expenses of life with two little boys and another baby on the way. Michael's stepdad called and offered us a loan, which Michael quickly said no to because we didn't want to burden them with our financial struggles. But after twenty-four hours, we called back and humbly asked for the loan. Michael knew that our first contract was in the works. Although we wouldn't be paid for another six months, we knew the money was coming. We used that loan to live another six months and paid his stepdad back with interest as soon as we received our first paycheck. Michael, being the godly man he is, was not trying to take any advantage of the generous offers he was given by these two men, my dad and his stepdad. By the time we got paid by MD7, it had been eighteen months since MD7 started. It was so sweet, and we were beyond grateful and thankful for this new income. God always sees us through and always has a way.

> *For the Lord your God has blessed you in all the*
> *work of your hand. He knows your trudging through*
> *this great wilderness. These forty years the Lord your*
> *God has been with you; you have lacked nothing.*
> DEUTERONOMY 2:7

It was September 2004 when we received our first paycheck from MD7. Day after day, MD7 grew, and prayers were heard and answered. We celebrated so many wins. God sustained us and gave us bigger and better contracts, and the employee headcount doubled. God had been with us and in every little detail from the start of this company. Like I already said, the provision of the Lord on MD7 has been an incredible journey and should be written into a book. We have witnessed and experienced stories that remind us that God is God and we are not, over and over again.

HONEY NUGGET

When God builds the foundation, no setback can shake the future He has planned for you.

CHAPTER 13

OUR MIRACLE BABY

Our third baby was born three months premature at twenty-seven weeks and five days. He was a measly two pounds, three ounces, born with a zero Apgar score. In layman's terms, he was born lifeless—not breathing, no heartbeat, not moving, not responding, and his skin was a dull, murky shade of gray. I wasn't supposed to go into labor that early, but I did, and here he was.

Ryan reminded us that life is precious, that every life is fragile and not guaranteed. I did not see my baby when he was delivered as he was whisked away at a frantic speed by a slew of specialists, technicians, and NICU nurses. The room went from being filled with the sounds of beeping machines, chaotic orders, and below-the-breath conversations just low enough to not make out what was being said but loud enough to understand the message that my newborn son's prognosis was not good—to deafening silence.

He was gone from my sight.

I was alone.

I missed the post-labor routine most moms experience when the doctor should have laid him on my chest so I could hold him for the first time. I did not get to kiss him, stare at him, or snuggle him. I did not get to look him in the eyes and tell him the one thing I had been holding in: "I have been waiting for you for so long."

Instead, three long and agonizing hours later, they pushed my hospital bed into the NICU (Neonatal Intensive Care Unit), where he was lying in an incubator with more tubes and wires hooked up to him than we could imagine. All I could hear were the alarms and beeping noises that were connected to life support machines, alerting everyone within earshot that my son was not breathing on his own. His body was so tiny, and nothing can prepare you to see your child barely holding on to life. The hospital staff tried to warn us, but seeing it with your eyes is another thing entirely. I had no words; Michael had no words. We were stunned and in complete shock. We looked at Ryan in silence while giant tears rolled down our faces. Our little son was fighting for his life while we were helpless and couldn't do anything to help him.

Oh, Jesus.

Ryan's head was as big as my fist, and his arms were the size of my index fingers. He did not look like a baby. His skin was almost transparent, and he had blue bruises in the shape of thumbprints on both shins from the doctor pulling him out of me. We could stick our overly sanitized hand into the incubator to lightly touch him, but we weren't able to hold him, kiss him, or do any of the everyday newborn things for weeks. His diaper was 3" x 3." It was so tiny because he was so tiny.

My body went into labor at twenty-four weeks this time, the absolute earliest of all three boys and too early for a guaranteed healthy birth. Each time I was pregnant I went into labor earlier than the last pregnancy. With Ryan, my third pregnancy, I was barely even showing. My bump was just big enough that I had put on maternity clothes for the first time two weeks prior. I began having what felt like menstrual cramps, something I knew I should not have. I called the doctor, went straight to the hospital, and never left.

I was put on hospitalized bed rest and had been at Scripps La Jolla for about ten days when the doctor came into my room (which I hadn't left except once for a sonogram down the hall). He said I was in labor again after looking at my numbers on the monitor. Because it was so early, they didn't want me to deliver at their hospital because they didn't have a Level 3 NICU (which provides critical care for babies born before thirty-two weeks). Ryan was still under one and a half pounds and would need a much higher level of care than Scripps could provide. They put me in an ambulance and sent me to the Hillcrest Medical Center at UC San Diego Health. Talk about stress and worry. Scared, I lay in the new hospital room alone with tears streaming quietly down my cheeks. Labor subsided after I arrived, and that was the only bright side to a dismal and sad situation. I was twenty-seven weeks along, but the goal was to keep the baby inside until thirty-seven weeks. I had two and a half more months to spend in the new hospital that was far from my home, my husband, and my two little boys.

Six days after arriving at the new hospital, labor started again, and this time, there was no stopping it. The doctors had tried everything they could to stop the labor, but nothing could. It was a Friday night, and Michael had just touched down after being away on a business trip. I was waiting impatiently for him to get to the hospital, and he came straight from the San Diego airport to my room. Things were getting serious, and I could not do this alone. The doctors came in to talk and try to prepare us for what was ahead, but there was nothing to prepare us for what we experienced.

Before going into the delivery room, they wanted to do a sonogram to check on the baby. They thought he was about two pounds now and found that he had flipped around 180 degrees and was breech. He was so small he could spin around and move wherever he liked. Ryan was like a little fish in a big fish tank because it isn't until around thirty-five weeks that babies get into the birthing position. Our little two-pound baby was feet first instead of head first, which meant another cesarean section. I didn't care about myself; I wanted the best for the baby. But it just added to the already hard situation. Instead of the delivery room, I was on my way to the operating room.

The night was awful. There was nothing similar to when Jake was born after hours of somewhat normal labor or when Luke was born via emergency C-section. They delivered Ryan in under thirteen minutes. However, this C-section was under very different circumstances. We were warned there was no guarantee of a successful delivery with a micro-preemie. It was like entering a dark, dismal tunnel with no light yet being told to find your way. Go. Now. You can't stop, turn, or go back, but you do not know what is ahead. It was all unknown and scary, and I felt claustrophobic. Everything was out of control, and there was nothing we could do.

During the procedure, I could feel the pain of the C-section. They had to call the anesthesiologist back in to administer a high dose of anesthesia, and then the doctor struggled to get the baby out. I picture Ryan holding on to something in there and fighting the exit. Like a dog playing tug of war with a toy trying to get you to let go, but you both hold on tight, pulling it back and forth. It felt violent as I lay there helpless. It seemed like everything was wrong, and nothing was going how it was supposed to go. The whole situation was bad. There was no joy, no celebration of a new baby being born. The operating room was eerily quiet, sterile, cold, and serious. The doctors and nurses quietly spoke to each other, and we were left to wonder what they were saying and what it all meant.

The only good thing that night was Michael. He was my rock, standing by my head and talking me through the devastation. That vow we took at our wedding when we said, "For better or for worse," well, that very late Friday night that turned into Saturday just after midnight was my "worse." I lost it. I was exhausted and weak and felt the weight of so much loss. My body had given out, and I felt a hundred percent guilty for it. Michael standing by my head during the C-section was the only way I got through it. I couldn't have done it without him speaking truth over me and encouraging me through every minute.

We had a sonogram at the last hospital to check on the baby just a few weeks before this night. He was just over one pound and growing, so we were happy. At the same time, we tried to NOT find out the sex of the baby this third time and let it be a surprise. When we told the technician our wish and that we had two boys at home, she went straight for the groin, and both Michael and I saw our third baby was a BOY. After they wheeled me back down the long hall to my hospital room, I looked at Michael and said, "I think I know what we are having." He said, "Me too!" We kissed and had a sweet moment, knowing that God had chosen another boy for us, and we were elated. Remember how I told you that story about Jake leaning in to kiss me in the kitchen? That day, in my mind, I also said, "Lord, if I could have all boys like this one, I would." I truly believe He heard me.

We didn't have a name picked out the night Ryan was born as we thought we had more time, at least two more months, to decide. We had just played around with a few names. During this time, my husband was boots on the ground starting up the new company. MD7 was an official company just two months prior to that night, so you can only imagine the chaos in our lives. New business, two babies at home and one on the way and way sooner than we had planned, and I had been in the hospital for weeks. We were hanging on by a thread. So, needless to say, when we unexpectedly went into labor for real, we had not finalized his name. During the hours of us waiting to go see our third son after he was delivered, we decided on RYAN, a favorite name of mine since … forever. Do you remember the movie *Sixteen Candles*? If you do, you know where I am going—Jake Ryan. I had our Jake, and Michael thought it would be weird to name Luke, Ryan, so bingo, third baby equals Ryan! I insisted he be named after Michael for his middle name since he helped me through the worst night of my life. We gave him Michael's middle name, David. We named him Ryan David—perfection!

While I was in the hospital, our precious friend Barry called me to share a Scripture he had prayed for Ryan and wanted us to know about it. This verse is the promise I held onto and begged the Lord to be faithful with. He says God never goes back on His Word. He keeps all His promises, so I held onto this promise for Ryan like I was hanging onto the wings of a plane in flight and my life depended on me not letting go. In my Bible, I wrote in Ryan's name, and I have read and prayed this verse over this child a thousand times over:

Fear not, for I am with you [Ryan];
Be not dismayed, for I am your God [Ryan].

I will strengthen you [Ryan],
Yes, I will help you [Ryan],
I will uphold you with My righteous right hand [Ryan].
Isaiah 41:10

Driving away from the hospital and leaving Ryan there for the first time, a few days after he was born, I thought my heart was being torn into two pieces. It was horrible and my worst nightmare. This dismal situation hurt me to the inner depths of my soul to the point of physical pain in my chest. Having my boys was my dream. So when that dream crashed and the part I had been waiting for, the part where I would be able to hold him, feed him, and take care of him was stripped away, I almost could not function. But I held onto Isaiah 41:10 like no other. All I could do was pray. I pleaded with the Lord:

> *Lord, You promise You will be with Ryan and help him. I can't do it. You have to do it. Please strengthen him and hold him because I can't. Help him grow and get strong so he can come home to us.*

We went back to the hospital every day to see Ryan and bring them breast milk I was pumping every three hours around the clock. He didn't have the ability to digest breast milk yet, and it would be weeks before he would have it via a Gavosh tube, but until then, we kept a steady supply on hand so that he would have it when his little body could start to digest it. I called the NICU every three hours for updates while I was at home with the boys. It was always a challenge to get to the hospital every day since I was unable to drive because of the C-section and I had two boys at home. So I not only needed a babysitter for Jake and Luke, but I also needed a driver to take me thirty minutes to the hospital. Michael was very busy start-ing his company, so it was a challenge—Every. Single. Day. So we did our best one day at a time. We made it work, but the days were long and hard. It was a battle, and one of the hardest times in my life.

During one of the first few days Ryan was in the NICU, a techni-cian came to do a sonogram of his brain to look for brain bleeds. *Oh, this is just fantastic*, I thought. Now he gets to have the horrific issue of brain bleeds and brain issues. The problems these little preemies face are just too much. I stood next to his incubator as they scanned and collected data. The doctors reported he had a significant brain bleed on the right side. Ooomph! My heart was heavy. My little baby would most likely have lifelong issues due to his premature delivery. Again, the weight of that was on me.

I felt hopeless and so frustrated, replaying everything that had happened up until he was born. I wanted a different outcome and wished I had done things differently. Maybe I could have refused to move to the new hospital or I could have demanded more meds or I could have skipped the only shower I took in those few weeks or maybe I could not have pushed that heavy cart in Costco. My mind went wild. I didn't want this outcome for my son. I would take it from him in a second if I could, but I couldn't. What could I do? I felt so out of control. After a few hours of pure torture, I landed on the thought that I needed to not only reach out to the God who is in control of everything but also ask others to reach out on Ryan's behalf.

I started calling all my family and friends. Email was new then, so I sent emails to people to pray for Ryan, asking them to pass on the requests to anyone who also prayed. Because of this brain bleed event, in my heart of hearts, I KNOW prayer changes things. The technician came back to recheck the brain bleed on the right side of his brain the following day, and you will not believe what you will read next. No brain bleed was suspected. Gone. Vanished. Zero. You see, God hears our every prayer, and He answers us. Prayer is powerful. God is powerful. My new mission was to pray, believe, and trust as I had a new hope and a new outlook on life for Ryan. Things could change, but I would be in communion with the God of the universe for Ryan.

To my surprise, when Ryan was six days old and we were in the NICU to visit him, the nurses asked if I wanted to hold Ryan for the first time. Here it was! The day I had dreamed about since he was just a twinkle in my eye. They had me open my shirt so he could lay on my skin. It is called Kangaroo Care, and studies have shown that babies thrive when connected to someone skin to skin. The first time I held him his little head fit right between my bosom. My bosom was actually bigger than his head; he was so tiny. Think of him as the size of a baby kitten. His skinny, little arms, legs, and body lay right on my skin. I could feel him moving ever so slightly. He felt like he did inside me again.

Oh my little man, I have missed having you this close to me so much.

Yes, you guessed it, tears would not stop coming from my eyes. I felt like I was finally able to connect with him, but I couldn't imagine what he was feeling. Once safe and warm and with his momma and then alone in a loud hospital NICU with a constant rotation of nurses and doctors caring for him with pokes and prods. Holding him was heaven on earth. My heart and soul were at peace, and I was finally reunited with him. I whispered to Ryan about how much

I loved and missed him as we rocked in the chair. I never wanted to let him go. I also told him how unbelievably sorry I was, as I was just so sorry. They allowed me to hold Ryan until his oxygen saturation got too low, and they had to get him back into his bed. In that time, I felt so happy to have three things I could do for him. I was able to pray, pump breast milk, and hold him skin to skin. He just needed to learn to breathe.

Ryan had good days and not-so-good days when he was in the hospital. It seemed he would make one step forward and then two back. Unfortunately, his breathing was always an issue. He was intubated for weeks, then toggled back and forth between a CPAP machine (which pushed air into his lungs but let him release it) and just simply oxygen. It was so hard to watch his little body lay there and fight to simply breathe. There was also the added stress of the fear of giving him too much oxygen because it would cause eye damage. They turned the oxygen up and down constantly, trying to give him enough but not too much, a constant battle.

During this time, Jake was three years old and in preschool at our church for a few hours three days a week. One day shortly after Ryan was born, he came home with his cute, little newsletter from his adorable preschool teachers. On it was the verse of the week. God knew I needed this verse as Ryan was still fighting for his life. It said,

Let everything that has breath praise
the Lord. Praise the Lord!
PSALM 150:6

"Yes, Lord!" I cried! Ryan does have breath, and You are supplying it for him. Praise You, Lord! Thank You that although he is on a ventilator, he has breath, and I am choosing to praise You!" I felt as though the Lord was speaking directly to me. He saw my deep concern and heaviness for Ryan. He touched me with this beautiful verse that calmed and reassured me that He saw and understood.

I had to choose to look for the good in the situation. If there is any good, it must be from God. But how was He showing up and making this horrible situation good? Most of what Ryan was dealing with was grave. Every day he fought. Every day we were challenged beyond what we ever thought we would be. But choosing to find and see the good and keeping our eyes fixed on Jesus were the only ways we would make it through. They were our only hope.

> *And we know that all things work together*
> *for good to those who love God, to those who*
> *are the called according to His purpose.*
> ROMANS 8:28

I long to be in His presence and by His side, hearing what He wants to say to me. I was on my knees praying for my baby and begging the Lord for His help.

> *As the deer pants for the water brooks, so pants my soul for*
> *you, O God, My soul thirsts for God, for the living God.*
> PSALM 42:1-2

Over the next three months, Ryan learned how to breathe independently, eat through his mouth instead of a tube, keep his temperature up, fight off infections, and gain weight. He needed to meet his preemie goals before he could leave the hospital. With

God's help and the medical doctors, nurses, and medicine, Ryan did it! He came home three months and one week (91 days) after the day of his birth, weighing six pounds even! God kept all His promises and was so faithful. He is trustworthy! During this storm, this nightmare, this dark tunnel, I had no choice but to walk through it. This absolutely solidified my faith. I had been on a journey seeking God and questioning Him to see if He was trustworthy. Well, it was decided once and for all. I will shout it from the mountaintops for the rest of my life!

GOD IS FAITHFUL AND TRUSTWORTHY. HE KEEPS ALL HIS PROMISES.

I have put my trust in the Lord God, that
I may declare all Your works!
PSALM 73:28

I will say of the Lord, "He is my refuge and my
fortress; my God, in Him I will trust."
PSALM 91:2

I love the Lord, because He has heard my voice and
my supplications. Because He has inclined His ear to
me, therefore I will call upon Him as long as I live.
PSALM 116:1-2

My faith was real; I trusted God with my life and everything else. I can confidently write that I am different because of this storm.

My flesh and my heart fail;
But God *is the strength of my heart*
and my portion forever!
PSALM 73:26 EMPHASIS ADDED

But God... is the answer to all of the brokenness.

But God... can heal the hurt.

But God... can make roses out of the ashes.

But God... can calm the winds and move the dark clouds
to create a beautiful day.

But God... can rebuild and repair after the devastation.

But God... can shine the brightest light into the darkness.

But God... is able to strengthen the weak.

But God... can illuminate any dark hallway.

But with God, we can do it and make it through this thing
we call life. God can do it.

Because of Him, I could weather the storm and come out safe.
He is my hope. He is my rock. He took what was awful and horrible
and made it good. He used this situation to solidify my faith. He did
miraculous work by strengthening Ryan. If you could only see and
know Ryan now. He is smart, strong, ridiculously handsome, completely healthy (minus asthma that runs on both sides of our families), and, most importantly, he loves the Lord with all his heart! You
would never guess he was two pounds when he was born. I see God's

goodness and faithfulness whenever I look at Ryan. He is a miracle. And I must say it again,

> *And we know that all things work together*
> *for good to those who love God, to those who*
> *are the called according to His purpose.*
> **ROMANS 8:28**

HONEY NUGGET

What begins as a season of tears can
end as a story of miracles when we trust
the One who keeps every promise.

CHAPTER 14

DREW, RENEE, AND RYAN

During the harshest storm I had ever been in, when Ryan, our third beautiful baby boy, was born three months premature and fighting for his life, there was another beautiful story being perfectly authored by God. It is a story that makes me smile and fills me with joy.

Before Ryan was born, I was in the hospital for three and a half weeks on bed rest. The doctors were doing their best to stop my labor, which had started at twenty-four weeks. They were incredible, and I am forever thankful for what they did to elongate my pregnancy and give Ryan three more precious weeks. Every twelve hours I would meet a new nurse who would take care of me hand and foot. They were all so sweet and knowledgeable, and I felt well cared for.

One of the nights Michael was able to leave Jake and Luke at home with my mom and come to the hospital to bring me a "feast" of non-hospital food and spend time with me. It was the best we could do to have our own little date night in the hospital. As we finished eating, the most beautiful blonde with the biggest smile walked in. She introduced herself as Renee, my night nurse for the next twelve hours. Michael engaged in conversation with her because of her Southern drawl, and they become entrenched in a discussion about Georgia, where she was from and where Michael had worked for a year. They chatted and laughed and carried on. She truly was the sweetest!

The minute she left the room, Michael immediately said, "Who can we set her up with?"

He loved her! I loved her!

"My brother, Drew!" I said without hesitation! They would be perfect.

Drew is sixteen months younger than I, and we have been best friends since we stopped trying to kill each other as young kids. I think we went from archenemies to best friends overnight in middle school. We figured out that we were better together than against each other. I am not kidding; he was my absolute best friend and confidant. I loved my brother and longed for him to have a wife so we could double-date and do life together. I was immediately on the phone to call him to get him up to the hospital. Drew explained he had just gotten home from working all day, had gone to the gym, and needed to shower. It was too late that night, but he asked me to find out when she worked again, and he would come up to Scripps Memorial Hospital in La Jolla for a visit. We never told Renee about my brother Drew; this was critical to the story unfolding.

A few days after we met Renee, I went into labor again, and the doctors didn't think they could stop it this time. They also didn't want to transport a micro-preemie to the NICU (Neonatal Intensive Care Unit) that was twenty minutes away from the hospital, so instead, they felt it was best to transport me to a new hospital while I was still pregnant. We had a few things on our minds, and let me just say that our matchmaking efforts were not at the top of them when we left Scripps.

Somehow, my labor calmed, and the baby had a few more days of growing inside before labor became uncontrollable again. It had been like a roller coaster ride, up and down every day for weeks. Between you and me, the ambulance ride, the physical move, the new medicines, and the emotional stress of the new hospital were what threw my body into labor for the final time. I was happy we moved hospitals to ensure the baby would be safer, but I was barely holding on. It was all too much, and that Friday evening, everything went south.

Our little miracle came just after midnight, so the night never seemed to end. It was dark, cold, and so scary. Nothing seemed good or joyful. In the morning, I called all of our family members to say our baby boy was born, and he was fighting for his life—please pray for him. When I talked to Drew, he was so kind and so concerned.

He then said, "I don't want to be inconsiderate of you and what is all going on, but what was the name of the nurse that you wanted me to meet last week?"

I said, "Renee."

He replied, "Heidi, I met her last night at Epazote in Del Mar."

What?! Are you kidding me? He went on to tell me the story. They each had gone out, begrudgingly, with a friend that night for dinner. They said they were both tired and only went not to break their promise to their friends. After dinner their companions were in no hurry to leave, so they ended up in the bar part of the restaurant. There was a college basketball game on the TV in the bar. The game was the icebreaker that initiated the conversation between them. Drew loves basketball, well actually all sports. Renee told him she went to Georgia and would be a forever Bulldog fan. Their conversation continued from there.

"What do you do?" Drew asked.

Renee said she was a labor and delivery nurse at Scripps La Jolla.

"Oh, my sister is in the hospital right now."

Renee asked, "Is she having a baby? Is she at Scripps?"

"She is actually trying not to have her baby, and no, she's no longer at Scripps."

"What's going on with her?"

As Drew was relaying the story, Renee said, "This sounds really familiar. I think I may have taken care of your sister. What's her name?"

"Heidi, Heidi Gianni," Drew offered.

"I did take care of your sister! I remember her. She was at Scripps but had to transfer to UCSD because she was threatening to deliver and was so high risk."

Drew didn't say a word about our phone call regarding him coming up to the hospital for a "visit" to meet this nurse Michael and I loved while she was on shift. He continued the conversation with her that night, wondering if this was the nurse we had called him about. That very hour and night, I was rushed into the operating room.

Do you see it? Do you see the goodness over the horror? I do. I see God on the throne. I see Him working good out of the bad and see His love and faithfulness shining so brightly.

God was on the throne, loving us and making roses out of ashes. He is so good because He literally took the worst night of my life and coupled it with my brother meeting his future wife on the same night!

And we know that all things work together
for good to those who love God, to those who
are the called according to His purpose.

ROMANS 8:28

Thank You, Jesus! Thank You for Your goodness! Thank You for loving us so well and having amazing plans for us and for Drew and Renee to meet. They went on their first date one week later and said they knew this was it. They both knew they had met the person they wanted to spend the rest of their life with. We tried to set them up that first night in the hospital, but God ultimately set them up to meet one week later at Epazote, the same night Ryan was born. They were engaged a few days after Ryan turned one, and now they have three beautiful children and the sweetest life together.

Clearly, You are a God who works behind
the scenes, God of Israel, Savior God.
ISAIAH 45:15 MSG

So what have you gone through? What hardships have you endured? Have you seen the goodness in them yet? Ask the Lord to show you and to bring it to your mind. My dream of having children was twisted and stopped short with all of my boys being born prematurely, but I was determined to find the good in it. A healthy life does not work in the "what-ifs" and "why me?" Instead, I had to switch my perspective to the fact that God is bigger than the worst nightmares and the horrible things that happen here on earth.

The Lord says:

These things I have spoken to you, that in Me you may
have peace. In the world, you will have tribulation
[trouble]; but be of good cheer, I have overcome the world.
JOHN 16:33

God knows. He sees. He cares. He says, "I see the fallen world and all the troubles you are going through, but hang tight to Me because I have overcome the world." He is bigger and better and has won the battles for us. Cling to Him and know He is trustworthy, loving, and working all things out for good for those who love Him. What if we looked at life through this lens? How different we would live. We would live in freedom and security, knowing that the Lord loves us and can make good out of the ugly, and He is always at work, even if we don't see Him at the moment.

HONEY NUGGET

Even in our darkest storms, God is quietly weaving beauty from the ashes, proving His love by turning our pain into unexpected joy.

CHAPTER 15

MOVING ACROSS THE POND

We moved to London in 2007.

Those six simple words hold enough weight, chaos, and change to fill an entire novel. Our G5 family, Michael, me, and our three boys, Ryan (4), Luke (5), and Jake (8), packed up our entire lives and left everything familiar: our lifelong home, our beloved extended family, every friend, our church, our neighborhood, our school, our routines, our comfort.

We boarded a twelve-hour flight from San Diego with far too many suitcases stuffed with clothes, necessities, books, toys, and games, actually anything we thought might make life feel normal again. We landed in a city we'd only visited a handful of times, where we were most certainly not citizens, and moved into a rental house so empty we had to rent every single thing. We rented furniture, dishes, linens, and the works, just to function.

And why? To build a home and a life for our family while expanding MD7 into the UK. It was bold and felt crazy, but this adventure was because we were following what the Lord asked us to do.

Mark Christenson, Michael's third employee at MD7 back in 2003, had become far more than a trusted colleague over the years. He was not only Michael's right-hand man in business but also his closest friend in life. When we made the move to London, Mark and his wife, Carolynn, made it too, bringing along their two little girls, Hannah, just two years old, and baby Clare, only three months old. Hats off to them because it was no small feat.

Looking back, it feels almost wild that we all pulled it off. There were nine of us in total, and when we paraded through the streets of London together, it must have been quite a sight that was chaotic but for us was absolutely unforgettable. We managed it only through the Lord's provision and strength and because we were young enough to be fearless and determined enough not to quit.

The Christensons lived just down the street from us, and for the first six weeks, we ate dinner together every single night. Those meals became the anchor of our day. We all shared stories, laughs, and encouraged each other through the challenges of building a new life overseas. Carolynn and I clung to one another during the days, tag-teaming childcare, and tackling the most basic tasks, like figuring out where the nearest grocery store was. They were true lifesavers in more ways than we could ever count, and their friendship turned what could have been an overwhelming transition into one of the richest seasons of our lives.

Although I say it was rich, it was also a lot for us, to say the least. There was so much to do, not only physically but emotionally. We all would agree that our time in London was a life-changing experience that has shaped us in many ways into the people we are today, even our children. Isn't that how it always is, though? In the adventures and challenging times we grow, change, and become better versions of ourselves if, and only if, we let them.

We tried to fight the change for a while, but then we all succumbed and embraced it. We no longer counted the days to go back home, but rather, we counted the blessing of being there. Before we arrived at counting all the pretty, little blessings, our G5 family all had our own challenge to meet. Michael's happened six weeks after we arrived in London. Our move to London was for a contract that was supposed to be our first work for MD7 in the UK. However, it was canceled before it was even signed. Ooph! That was supposed to be the footing for us to start expanding through the UK. So it was a huge disappointment when he received the bad news as that was the sole purpose of nine people moving there. Michael's valley led him to dig in deep and figure out what we would do in a new country without the contract. I can't wait to share how God took this disappointment and made it into something far better than we could have ever imagined for MD7.

The valley I was in was the I-Am-All-Alone Valley that some of you also know. The boys were all in school for the first time, my husband was gone all day, we had moved to a foreign city where I didn't drive, and it was very unlike my home city. I was so thankful for Carolynn but was definitely challenged with none of my other friends there. To add to it, my stay-at-home mom job had a vast duty change that I had chosen to ignore for years. I thought my kids would be in diapers and need me to feed them, and nurture them forever. Oopsie! That was not the case. My identity was being challenged like it had never been before. I had literally worked myself out of a job. Why did

I teach them how to feed themselves, how to put on a pair of pants, and how to walk? Why? Why? Why? I am kidding as I say this and trying to be funny here, but seriously, my success in training the boys up was to my own demise. I can't wait to show you how my challenge turned out to be one of the best gifts of my life!

My boys' challenge was the uncomfortable situation of being in a new school and a foreign land. They were not excited about their new school situation, which differed vastly from their school back home. They begged daily to move back to San Diego.

The easy thing would have been to move back to San Diego by fixing our pain and not pressing into our situation. It would have solved all of our problems in an instant. But the Lord clearly had led us there so why would we give up so quickly. So we didn't give up. Instead of packing up, Michael and Mark took the denial of this contract in England, looked up to the Lord, and asked Him what to do. Michael didn't blame God or ask Him why this was happening. No, he said, "What is God directing us to do next?" So my go-getter husband started researching and finding all the other clients and customers he could in Europe. It was another long road to get our first contract, but with God's direction and grace, he did it. The seeds planted for MD7 in those years are now flourishing offices all over Europe. He just opened his seventh office this year, and it was because of the setback that the comeback was even sweeter. God has been so faithful to us and kept all His promises with MD7.

Meanwhile, I dug in deep with the boys' school. They were my life, so I might as well join them. I met with all the teachers and the headmaster, bought the literacy curriculum for our home, scoured through all the school's papers I could read, and investigated the school and its policies. I knew too much as an educator, and we were talking about my most precious people—my boys. As all moms do, I wanted only the best for them. Unfortunately, it turned out that we did not fit into this school. I am sure this school was amazing for the British kids who had been in their school system from the beginning, but for foreigners, it was not, and it was obvious after only the first month. We planned to be in London for only one year, so I was nervous I would be "messing up their year." So after a few weeks of "dropping my kids off at the lions' den" (I very appropriately called it behind closed doors), I became very concerned.

Every day, there was more evidence that the schoolwork did not fit our children. I felt like it was the classic Goldilocks story: One boy was in a grade too high, one was in one too low, and one was just right. I did my best to help them after school by augmenting their work to fit their needs, but as the first semester came and went, I could see the destruction. Jake was literally being pulled out of class and put into a non-English speaking group to help him with his schoolwork, even though he spoke perfect English. They had placed him in a grade level higher than he had been educated because of his summer birthday. Next, Luke refused to go to school (see chapter 16, "Scripture in Your Pocket") because he was already reading and doing double digit adding and the grade level was teaching him his letters and sounds and how to count to eleven. Not where this child needed to be either. To top it off, we also had social issues due to our American accents and blonde hair. Yes, Jake was referred to as "Jake Beverly Hills," which he did not like at all. Yes, it is funny to us now, but to an eight year old, it was not. Ryan was great though; he loved his appropriate grade that they put him in. He and I spent half of his day together since he was only in school until just before lunch.

Here is what the Lord was up to: Michael had an early morning breakfast with some faithful, God-loving friends he had met in London through a connection he had through YWAM. They discussed Scripture that showed Michael the Lord was faithful and would protect us during this very uncomfortable time with his business and our personal life. He came home and read it to me because he resonated with the verse so much and felt like God was reassuring him about our tough situation. He sat on the edge of the bed and read from his Bible to me. It said,

> *For he shall give his angels charge over you,*
> *To keep you in all your ways.*
> *In their hands they shall bear you up,*
> *Lest you dash your foot against a stone.*
> **You shall tread upon the lion and the cobra,**
> **The young lion and the serpent**
> **you shall trample underfoot.**
> *Because he has set his love upon Me,*
> *therefore I will deliver him;*
> *I will set him on high because he has known My name.*
> *He shall call upon Me, and I will answer him;*
> *I will be with him in trouble;*
> *I will deliver him and honor him.*
> *With long life I will satisfy him,*
> *Aand show him my salvation.*
>
> PSALM 91:11-16 EMPHASIS ADDED

My heart just stopped. The lion reference got me! I had been saying it day after day; I felt like I walked them to school every morning and "dropped them off in the lions' den." The Lord says, "Yes, you will tread upon a lion and have trouble, but I am trustworthy to help you." Then the Lord just poured in the peace and comfort, saying He knew it would be hard and difficult, but He was with them. He would protect them while they were "in the lions' den." He would deliver them. I felt God was saying, "I have got them, and I have a plan!" The boys continued at the Goldilocks of a school, and the Lord was with them and preparing their minds and hearts for their future.

HONEY NUGGET

Even in the deepest valleys and most uncertain seasons, God turns setbacks into sweeter comebacks and walks with us every step, faithfully protecting and guiding us toward His greater plan.

SCRIPTURE IN YOUR POCKET

We have all had days when life is hard, right? We want to stay in bed, pull the covers back over our heads, and not face what we know lies outside our bedroom door. Well, picture a day like that, but it is your upset five year old who says he doesn't want to go to school, and by his tone and persistence, you know it's serious. My little, sweet-faced son Luke was begging me to let him stay home. This was not like him at all as he loved school. He was always eager to learn and dove into anything, whether it was school, a new team sport, or a birthday party, headfirst with excitement. So I knew something was wrong.

I listened to him sob and try to convince me to let him stay home. Also, I was trying to diagnose what was wrong but needed to be out the door within minutes with Luke and his brothers. If you have kids, you know the crazy, wild mornings getting ready for school. Getting them out of bed, getting dressed, having breakfast, making lunches, and finding the other shoe that, for some reason, is never in the same vicinity as the first shoe.

Luke repeated over and over that he didn't want to leave me and just wanted to stay home. I needed to figure out what to do, but whatever it was, I needed to do it quickly! I asked God what to do in my head as I listened to him. The Holy Spirit prompted me to tell my son Philippians 4:13:

I can do all things through Christ who strengthens me.

I said, "Luke, Jesus will be with you all day, and He will help you. He will make you strong, and you will be able to do it." I then said, "Why don't I write out the Scripture, and we will put it in your pocket so every time you need help, you can touch the paper and be reminded of God's promise to you?" I must say the Holy Spirit is so creative and makes a way. Luke made it through the day, the next day, and the next. I was hoping to teach him that I was not his only comfort and strength, but he also had access to comfort, love, peace, direction, and strength from the Lord. He is the constant who will never leave or forsake him. Oh, I do want to be that for Luke and all my boys and my husband, but I can't. I can't do what God only can do. I can't always be there. I won't always know the answers or what to do. But like us all, we will experience these emotions, hard events, struggles, challenging days, and tough seasons.

There is no doubt Luke will be afraid, sad, lonely, and frustrated, but the Lord is his answer. He can do it with Him. I was hoping he learned that sometimes we have to do things we don't feel like doing. However, God is trustworthy and is his strong tower who is there for him no matter what. He just needs to reach out and ask. Luke learned to be resilient and to get back up again when we are knocked down because this life is hard.

I finally did find out what was bothering Luke. He was in a class at the Goldilocks school that was leveled too low for him, so he was bored, not challenged, and not learning. He is a gifted student, but I didn't realize this was the problem at this point. The Lord was at work orchestrating a million little things that changed everything about our family, education, and plan that we thought was made. No, the Lord had something so much better, and we were about to walk into the next chapter together as a family.

HONEY NUGGET

Even when we feel scared, unready, or alone, God's strength is our constant companion that is equipping us to face what's ahead and leading us with every step we should take.

CHAPTER 17

RESCUE MISSION

Sometimes, God sends a boat, helicopter, or lifesaver out of nowhere to get us out of a situation and "save" us from the valley we are in. One time God did a crazy thing to get us out of our valley that we never could have planned or expected; that is what makes life so exciting and fun—the adventure of the plans the Lord has made. This is how the first part of the rescue unfolded.

While we were living in London, Michael had business meetings in Italy, so he left early one morning, planning to be gone for a few days. As he left London's Heathrow Airport, authorities told him they would not let him back into England before he was fingerprinted and finalized all the paperwork in America for his work visa. He called me from Heathrow that morning after I had just walked the boys to school and was at the grocery store. "Sweet Cheeks, you need to pack up the boys and meet me in Los Angeles tomorrow; otherwise, you could be deported."

I put all the food from my grocery cart back and hustled home. I made travel arrangements and packed up the boys, and we were off to LA the following day where we would meet Michael after he flew from Italy to LA. It was a clear adventure that we had not anticipated or planned! We were going "home" for the first time since we left four months prior. The boys were on their absolute best behavior, and I was so proud of flying twelve hours back to the United States alone with the three of them. We were all giddy with joy! *Okay, God, what are You up to?* I thought. We had buckled down and tried to get our stride in London, and we had all moved forward to embrace it there. And poof, we were yanked out (or I would like to say rescued) with less than twenty-four hours of notice.

It was glorious to be back in San Diego with all of our family and friends! Because it was a few weeks before Christmas, it was perfect timing to stay and enjoy our K19 family. What is K19, you ask? Well, it is the best little family, the Kleis family, that I get to be a part of, which includes my dad, Henry (or Hank), and my mom, Susan. I am the oldest of the five children. I have two brothers and two sisters and don't ask how my mom and dad had a girl, boy, girl, boy, and girl but they did! Drew, my brother, his wife Renee, his children, Carter, Katie, and Hailey; my sister Gretchen, her husband Brent, and boys Brady and Grayson; my brother Markus and wife Ashley; and my sister Heather. That makes nineteen, not counting any dogs or cats. That is my K19 family and my most cherished people with whom I have the privilege of doing life. Christmas was especially sweet because we were all united again. We used to have family meals and gatherings every Sunday, so being together filled our hearts to overflowing.

After Christmas, we had a few snags trying to return due to Michael traveling again for business and the paperwork, so honestly, we were relishing being home with everything familiar. There is comfort in the familiar. We could temporarily forget our individual valleys while we were home in San Diego with our people and routine. The boys needed to be back in school, but we still didn't have a return flight back to London.

One of my best friends, Leasha, knew of our situation with the boys and their Goldilocks school in London. She and I had met years before and became immediate friends and did absolutely everything together. We were both teachers in El Cajon at Meridian Elementary School. When we met, she was married but had no kids yet, and I was single. We experienced so much together as I got married, and we had three children each. She had three girls, and I had three boys. She later adopted a fourth daughter from Ethiopia. It was quite fun and so adorable to get all of our kids together as you can imagine all these little ones out and about. Leasha and I both earned our master's degree in Curriculum and Instruction from San Diego State University while we were still teaching elementary school. She finished one summer before me because I had little sweet Jake and couldn't finish my third summer of classes with a newborn. I finished the following summer when Jake turned one. She and I talked about everything every day, multiple times a day! We were wives together, moms together, teachers together, and she was also a Jesus lover, so we had that together.

I looked up to her for so many reasons—she was not only a stellar wife and mom but one of the best teachers I had ever worked with. When her girls were born, she left the classroom to be a full-time mom. As they approached school age, she decided to home-school them. You see where this is going, right?

This was the other half of the rescue, the life-saving ticket that God provided to lead us to leave the British school and all of the problems we were having there and homeschool the three boys. I could teach the boys at the grade level they needed and augment the curriculum that challenged them and educated them at the level that would accelerate their learning. It saved me as well, in the most wonderful way by giving me a new challenge and purpose using what I loved, teaching, for my boys. It was a double blessing for the boys and me. Leasha was my greatest cheerleader, always ready to help with homeschooling. I knew God had placed her in my life for many reasons, and this was yet another. She was right there beside me. I could see the Lord's hand in every detail of this new chapter of our lives.

The homeschooling experience was instrumental in our lives. To this day, I cherish every moment that we had in our converted living room. I set up a full working classroom which included desks, a reading corner, a full solar system hanging from the ceiling, charts, a whiteboard, etc. I used their previous school as a model for the curriculum I would choose for them so when we did return to San Diego, they could walk right back into their classes and not skip a beat. God knew my heart and knew what would set them up for success in their educational career. Homeschooling not only taught them the various curriculum, but it also made these three brothers into best friends. And this is still true, eighteen years later. I also think it taught them how to be self-starters, think of others above themselves, have perseverance, and understand that hard work pays off, to name a few of the thousands of benefits they gained that I had a front row seat to witness.

Personally, I learned how to be more patient and not be so uptight and control every little detail of my house. You see, I love to have everything clean and organized and in its place. I love a beautiful meal on the table, candles lit, soft music playing to provide a peaceful atmosphere. When you homeschool in your living room, you must let go of a few things: correction, most things! There just isn't enough time or capacity to have everything clean and perfect all the time. I changed my priorities to school, learning, and the souls of these kids: Dishes could wait, and laundry could wait. Homeschooling the boys was my new focus, and I was determined to do it the best I could.

I was also elated to use my master's degree and new knowledge on my OWN boys, since they were my students now. I still can't believe how that worked out! God is doing this all day, every day, in our lives. I had to open my eyes and look for it, hunt for the honey, per se.

I could have easily complained and been annoyed with the fact that I graduated when Jake was one year old and I was no longer teaching. I could have said, "What a waste of time." Instead, I finished my degree and was glad I did it only because I trusted in God's plan. I knew He would not waste all those journals and studies I read, all the endless projects and the papers I wrote. I could have missed this opportunity without looking for it, without knowing God was up to something good.

Homeschooling was amazing, and I loved it, but I was looking for a little encouragement. I needed a little word from the Lord to stand on. This is really funny how I found the verse when I look back on it. I searched on the internet for answers from the Bible to the question: Should parents teach their children at home? I am laughing at myself now thinking about what I wrote in the search engine hoping to get an answer. But I was really desperate to know if what I was doing was single-handedly "ruining" my own children. Haha! The internet showed me the answer: Deuteronomy 6:5-7.

> *You shall love the Lord your God with all your heart, with*
> *all your soul, and with all your strength. And these words*

> *which I command you today shall be in your heart. You shall*
> *teach them diligently to your children, and shall talk of them*
> *when you sit in your house, when you walk by the way, when*
> *you lie down, and when you rise up.*

I lost it. This was it! Homeschooling is just this—it is teaching and pouring into your children from dawn to dawn. Whether we were in the schoolroom during school or not, I was teaching, and they were learning every moment we were together. This Scripture is what I held in my heart, and I read it anytime I felt uneasy about the path we were on. This was the Scripture that gave me direction and peace so I could be confident in what I was doing.

To top it all off, I looked in my precious Bible to read it from the book instead of the screen, and what did I find? You will not believe this. On the side of those exact verses, it says, "Read at wedding 10/3/98." It had been nine years since God's Word was read aloud and over us at our wedding. God knew even before we did that I would homeschool our children and this Scripture would be meaningful to me when I needed encouragement and direction most.

The other unbelievable thing was, guess who read that Scripture at our wedding? Yes, you guessed it: Leasha! That is how big and mighty and wonderful God is. He orchestrates and works at all times. I marvel at who He is, and I love seeing glimpses of Him at work. This is the honey, the sweetness of God.

I must ask you now how is God orchestrating and working in your life? How is He tying the details of your life together into a beautiful, wrapped, packaged gift to encourage you and ground you? I hope this story will show you how mighty He is and how He can bind all these fragmented pieces together.

I still thank Him for helping me finish my master's degree even when I was a stay-at-home mom and thought it was a waste. I thank Him for the name-calling at the British school that left my son fearful of the teasing and even for the mix-ups that placed two of my boys in classes determined by their ages rather than their actual grade levels. The mismatch, though frustrating at the time, became part of the story He was writing for us. The things that looked unfair and wrong God took and turned into something so beautiful (Romans 8:28). I thank Him for leading us to use that Scripture out of the thousands that could have been chosen at our wedding. I thank Him for having my sweet friend, whom I adore, to read the Scripture. I mean seriously, what else am I missing that I am not looking for in my life? He is always at work. I love Him, and I love hunting for glimpses of His sweetness at work.

HONEY NUGGET

The very valleys we long to escape often become the places where God plants His richest blessings.

CHAPTER 18

THE RED TULIP

I discovered a book called *Captivating: Unveiling the Mystery of a Woman's Soul* by John and Stasi Eldredge that helped me understand who I was as a woman and how God made me. I felt understood; by understood, I mean heard and seen. I felt like this book was written to me personally to answer all my questions about who I was as a woman. This book offered "precious wisdom on the path to becoming a woman."[3] After we put the boys to bed at night, I would soak in the tub and devour this book. I cannot recommend this book enough to better understand what it is to be a woman, whether it be for yourself or to understand a woman's heart.

This book helped me understand my soul, who I am deep inside and why God made me this way. We all know the expectations and pressure the world piles on women. Everywhere we turn, we're flooded with messages about what makes a "good woman" and what she should or shouldn't do. It can feel like a relentless uphill climb of constant striving, performing, and proving ourselves. For most of my life, the world told me I was getting it wrong. My struggle was that I measured myself against other women, especially the ones I saw in magazines and on social media, holding my worth up to their standard. But here's what I've learned: Comparison is not just unhelpful... it's fatal to the soul. Remember this if you tend to compare like me: "Compare-is-sin."

I wasn't looking at myself through God's eyes and how He created me unique and special—like every single person on this earth. I was longing and trying to be and striving to be someone else. I didn't realize I was doing this to my detriment. This book helped me truly understand my heart and my soul and what I desired most was to be *lovely.* Deep in a woman's soul she desires "to be romanced, play an irreplaceable role in a great adventure and to unveil beauty."[4] *Captivating* helped me see my uniqueness in how God made me and why. I have since read this book four times, and every time I finish it, I say how great it is and how I need to read it again. The men's version is called *Wild at Heart* by John Eldredege. It is equally as powerful for men to understand who they are and why God made them that way. Michael and my boys have all read this life-changing book.

I had always longed to be romanced, not only by my husband, but by God, though I didn't recognize that desire until I read this book. In her writing, Stasi Eldredge described God's personal pursuit of me, of you, in a way I had never before heard or understood. She wrote:

> Every song you love, every memory you cherish, every moment that has moved you to holy tears has been given to you from the One who has been pursuing you from

your first breath in order to win your heart. God's version of flowers and chocolates and candlelight dinners comes in the form of sunsets and falling stars, moonlight on lakes and cricket symphonies, warm wind, swaying trees, lush gardens, and fierce devotion. This romancing is immensely personal. It will be as if it has been scripted for your heart. He knows what takes your breath away, knows what makes your heart beat faster. We have missed many of his notes simply because we shut our hearts down in order to endure the pain of life. Now, in our healing journey as women, we must open our hearts again, and keep them open. Not foolishly, not to anyone and anything. But yes, we must choose to open our hearts again so that we might hear his whispers, receive his kisses.[5]

She shared the most fascinating story of the Lord showing himself to her husband John. He was walking on the beach on the Oregon coast and praying to God and just enjoying the time with Him. He sat down to really enjoy the ocean scene and the fellowship he was having with the Creator. Then all of a sudden an enormous whale jumped out of the water. It was like a kiss from the Lord.

Stasi then explained how she also wanted God to show her He heard her and that He loved her, but she thought there was no way that this would happen to her because she knew God loved John so much but believed He didn't love her that much.[6] Wow! I had the same feelings as Stasi. Why? God loves everyone so much; I can understand that, but when I thought about myself, I couldn't believe He loved me the same either. I was so hard on myself, looking inward instead of upward. It was not about who I was or what I had done or will do but rather who was God? What is His character? How does He love? How does He care?

Stasi continued with her story that she went for a walk on the beach to see if God would show her a whale. She walked and walked and saw nothing. After looking, asking, and walking the beach for over an hour and not seeing a single whale or even a splash of one she was feeling defeated. She was about to turn back and go home. She thought to herself that she would continue up to the big cliff ahead and then turn around. She peered around the corner of the cliff to see around it and "saw a vibrant orange starfish." She knew at once it was God's gift to her, "His kiss." Stasi said she knew immediately the whale was for John, but God gave her a stunning starfish.

God had answered her question and guess what God had for her next? He didn't show her one starfish but hundreds of colorful starfish all over the sand right at the water's edge! There were orange, purple, and blue starfish, all of different sizes covering the entire beach. It was breathtaking! The waves came up and slowly turned into a gentle flow of water that beautifully moistened the starfish so they glittered and glowed in the beaming sun. At that moment, Stasi was hearing and seeing the Lord answer her request. Being in God's presence like this is the most invigorating and life-giving feeling that touched her soul with "His kiss."[7]

I didn't think much of it at the time, though the idea of "seeing" God show me He heard me and loved me sounded intriguing. Honestly, I wasn't expecting anything—I just enjoyed hearing her stories. The thought of receiving a "kiss" from God felt unlikely, almost too personal to imagine. While I knew God was all-powerful, I hadn't considered that He might interact with me in such an intimate way. In many ways, I was like Stasi in that I believed God loved the world and others but was unsure why He would have time for someone like me. Not in a self-pitying way, but more in awe that God of the entire universe would have time for me, let alone be available to me kind of way. With that thought lingering in my mind, I climbed out of the tub, went to bed, and slept soundly through the night.

In the early morning I woke and snuggled up in my favorite place in the house, a window bench that overlooked the Thames River. I loved sitting there and reading my Bible before the boys woke up for school. After reading my morning devotional I would look up the commentary by Jon Courson in his amazing *Application Commentary* set. He literally takes every Scripture and explains it in everyday language and culture so we can understand it, adding little stories that are so powerful. If I ever read a Scripture and want more meaning, I go to Courson's commentaries. I learn so much from him and keep his books on my Kindle so wherever I am, I can refer to them. He also has great podcasts so I can listen to his wisdom and insights.

This particular morning, to my absolute surprise as I walked up to the window with my hot cup of coffee from downstairs, it had snowed in London. It was so beautiful! It rarely snowed in London, so this was a special treat, and I couldn't wait for the boys to wake up! I sat on a window bench and looked out; I could sit there for hours, just taking in all the busy morning that was waking up. The sky was a dark gray, the murky Thames River rolled by, and the air was calm. It was so beautiful on this early winter morning. On the far side of the river, people walked on a winding path. Huge black birds were perched high in the tree branches that had lost their leaves.

Boats passed by. It was calm and peaceful to look at this landscape as everything had a beautiful blanket of white over it! After a few moments of enjoying this beautiful snow and taking it all in, my gaze went down two stories below me to our own backyard. Here was how God spoke straight to my soul. Are you ready? I didn't ask God for what I wanted to see, nor had I ever asked God to even see anything. I was not hunting for anything or expecting to find anything either. I know now that God knew me and my inner depths of my deepest being when I looked out that window. To my astonishment and total surprise, ONE perfect red tulip had popped its head out of the newly fallen snow and was beaming its beautiful self for all of the garden and for me to see.

The Lord your God in your midst, the Mighty One,
will save; He will rejoice over you in gladness,
He will quiet you with His love,
He will rejoice over you with singing.
ZEPHANIAH 3:17

That beautiful tulip that showed up in the most unexpected and most wonderful morning was God saying, "I see you, Heidi. I understand you, and I made you just how you are. I love you." This encounter with the Creator and Sustainer of the universe who sees me, cares for me, and loves me regardless of my mistakes and my sins quieted me with His love. I was calm and confident in whom He made me to be, knowing that I was not alone. This was the most incredible truth that rocked my world. I was in a relationship and conversing with the King of all kings! My heart overflowed, and my confidence grew. Not because of who I am, because I am not worthy, but because of who He is and what He has done. He showed me that morning that I was worth speaking to. He was on the throne.

HONEY NUGGET

God delights in showing His love in the most personal and unexpected ways, reminding us that we are deeply seen, fully known, and endlessly cherished by Him.

CHAPTER 19

HIS PERFECT PLAN

I was educated to be a traditional teacher in the classroom and had loved every single day of my career from my first job in Cerritos, California in 1993 where I taught bilingual Spanish kindergarten until my very last day of teaching six years later to my first grade class in El Cajon, California in 1999. My students became a huge part of my life, and I loved them like they were my own.

Getting the chance to teach again in London was a dream come true, but there was one caveat: I was moving from the classroom to homeschooling. There was definitely a bit of a learning curve, but I tackled it head on and loved it. My three students were in three grade levels. Jake was in second grade, Luke was in kindergarten, and Ryan was in preschool. We had a lot of subjects to do every day, and I had to adjust the activities and expectations according to each boy's level. I am sure I didn't do it perfectly, but I sure tried. It was some of the hardest yet most rewarding work I had ever done.

When we first moved to London in 2007, we were only supposed to go for one year. Well, you guessed it, Michael said we would be staying in London another year after we finished the first one. I was also very grateful we were able to take each year at a time. It made staying palpable since it was such a big commitment to stay away from our family and friends and life at home.

After living there two years, Michael and I were in a great life routine and were on our weekly date nights. London is an awesome city, and we loved it! Tuesday nights allowed us to reconnect and have "adult" conversations to talk about our days together. I just loved being with him. Well, you won't believe this, but one night I asked him if we could please stay one more year so I could homeschool the boys for a third year. I was so in love with them, and we were making so much academic progress! He laughed because the roles had reversed, and I was the one asking him to stay. I was so excited to have another year in our little homeschooling room in our house and be with the boys!

The third year went fantastically well until the spring of 2010 when I saw some signs from Jake that he wasn't being challenged enough with me. He is a gifted student who loves school and learning and was just finishing fourth grade. Jake loved to read and excelled in all of his subjects, but he needed more than I was offering. I expressed my concerns to Michael, and he agreed that we should look into putting him back into school for the next year in London. The school we found after lots of research was the American School of London which was an hour drive from our home. Hmmm, I didn't drive. I mean, I did drive but not in London on the wrong side of the car and the wrong side of the road! We would have to move houses if we wanted Jake to switch to this school; that seemed like a hard thing to do after we had finally settled into our house and little town we loved. This was not ideal. But we still looked, inquired, and completed all the tedious applications and testing.

Here is what God was up to: The school we had chosen was unavailable that next year, but it would be available the following year in 2011. Oh dear! We didn't need school the following year; we needed it next year. I was so confused and so disappointed. I really thought I had found the path we needed to take for Jake. So one more year of homeschooling was ahead of us although I really had a deep conviction that he should be back in regular school.

We were at church at Holy Trinity Brompton in London the following Sunday. The boys were in their classes, and Michael and I were at the main service. We had a beautiful time of worship when I started praying and telling God how much I was trying to understand this roadblock in school. I had spent months researching and doing tours and applications. I really thought this American school was what we were supposed to do. At that moment, I heard the Holy Spirit say to me, "John 13:7." Off the top of my head, I had no idea what that verse said. I shuffled through the pages of my Bible and found the Scripture:

> *Jesus answered and said to him, "What I am doing you
> do not understand now, but you will know after this."*
> JOHN 13:7

Peace fell over me like a warm, heated blanket wrapped around me in the cold crisp night. I knew the Lord had spoken to me and told me to trust Him regarding the plans for the boys' education. I did not need to fret or worry or try to figure it out. He had a plan even if I didn't see it yet. I had direction straight from God through

His Word. That was all I needed at that point. God had revealed to me that He was at work and I needed to just trust Him.

Fast forward a few months, and it was summertime. We were in San Diego for a visit when Michael unexpectedly told me to look into getting the boys back to their Christian school that they had left three years prior because we were moving back to San Diego! This is what God was up to! He knew the whole time we would be moving back and the boys would all be back in traditional school. The hunch I had about getting Jake back in school was spot on, and the Lord had it covered. If I would have pressed ahead without His reassurance and direction, who knows what would have happened!

The Bible tells us that God cares for us deeply and has a specific plan and purpose for each of our lives. In my walk with Him, I've learned that I can bring Him every question and every thought— whether big or small. He reveals His plan in pieces, offering just enough for me to take the next step and keep moving forward in faith.

HONEY NUGGET

When God reveals His plan one step at a time, we can rest in knowing that every detail is already written and perfectly timed for our good.

CHAPTER 20

FREEDOM FROM LIES: ALL MEN CHEAT

I didn't know I was living in a prison, but I was. It was dark and dreary, with exceptionally high walls. With each passing day, my every move seemed more and more limited. The longer I lived in the cage, the smaller it got and the more it closed in—suffocating me. It affected me daily. My thoughts, actions, and feelings put my life in peril. The crazy thing is that I hadn't even realized that I was a prisoner because of the cage that held me, which I had created myself. My prison was in my mind, and what kept me incarcerated were the beliefs I had subscribed to, lies that I alone thought were truth. I walked around daily, existing in false narratives. Those narratives were tying me down and holding me back from the glorious freedom that I knew Jesus had already paid for me. He had already won the battle, yet I was still in the fight—*why was I still in the fight?*

The biggest lie I told myself was that my husband was destined to cheat on me. I grew up believing all men were unsatisfied with their wives so they cheated. The movies and shows I watched growing up glorified the mistress and made the wife look like a dull, homely rag. I believed this was a known and widely accepted fact, and it was only a matter of time before my husband saw me as that dull, homely rag. This lie made me insecure about who I was as a wife, convincing me I was never beautiful enough, smart enough, busy enough, or doing enough of all the things that would make me worthy of my husband.

I would see him—not in reality but vividly in my mind—driving with other women in his car during the day while I was home taking care of our three little boys. As any mother knows, those years are hard. I could barely get dressed, let alone be his "perfect" wife. I couldn't handle hearing about his work meetings with intelligent women and go-getter colleagues who were "killing it at the office." In my mind, I would imagine scenarios where these women would feel sorry for my husband having to be tied down to me. Pity parties would run in my head, thinking, *Wow, I am just a mom, and I'll never measure up to these beautiful, professional women*. Everything I did felt like a fight, an invisible battle for his attention and love. However, I often felt defeated because I thought it was inevitable that he would find someone better and leave me alone in my dull, homely rag-ness.

This story is hard to share as it is the deepest, darkest fear I had about myself and my marriage. The only reason I can now write about this and be vulnerable is because the Lord is so good. He healed me, and I was set free. When we decide to surrender and finally recognize the lie in us and then ask the Lord to help us, He will.

Then you will know the truth, and the truth will set you free.

JOHN 8:32 CEB

That freedom is indescribable and changes everything. We are free, the cage door is swung open, we can exit, and the lies are crushed. Jesus, our Lord, is our Savior. He holds the key to open the cage. He has already battled on our behalf, wrestled the key out of the devil's hand, and set us free. We have to believe Him and receive it.

What is the lie that's holding you? Does it have to do with your past? A deep hurt? A wound that left you devastated? I implore you to ask the Lord to help identify the lies or ask a trusted friend to help you identify them. We are almost always blind to the lies and sin in us—they are so close to us that we can't see them for what they are. Sin creates a cozy little place in our hearts, a place so close to us that we don't even recognize that it is there. Sin and lies steer our thinking and feelings, which, in turn, steer our actions—which affect our whole life. It can be so dangerous to give any credence to them.

I was doing Beth Moore's *The Inheritance* Bible study with three friends. One night I made an offhand comment about Michael: "He hasn't cheated yet, but I know he will." My friends went silent, froze, and stared back at me. I knew I had said something that wasn't resonating with them. They asked why I said that. Little by little, they exposed this thought I had deep inside me. They began probing more about him—probably to make sure I really wasn't being cheated on. And I wasn't. My statement was the furthest thing from reality. Michael went above and beyond to ensure he was never in a position to be accused of inappropriate behavior. He was always blameless and above reproach when it came to having to be in the presence of other women, never going to lunch or driving with one woman in the car; he always brought another person. I didn't even know he was aware of the danger, but my loving, faithful husband knew, so he safeguarded himself and our marriage against any temptations.

Why in the world was I living this way? The very lie that had ensnared me was the exact thing Michael was expertly tackling. He was doing everything he could to honor me. With that said, my friends gave me Scripture that night and asked probing questions about my marriage and my husband. They pointed me to the truth, which was right in front of me, helping me see that I was projecting past relationships, fictional characters, and our backward culture to my most loving and loyal husband. This is the verse I read and refer to often when I feel the lies beginning to intrude on my thoughts:

> *Finally, brethren, whatever things are true, whatever things are noble, whatever things are just, whatever things are pure, whatever things are lovely, whatever things are good report, if there is any virtue and if there is anything praiseworthy—meditate on these things.*
>
> PHILIPPIANS 4:8

What a fantastic verse for me to stand on!

> *Yes, Lord, thank You for Your living Word that can speak to me today! It is the living Word, and I am so grateful You gave us this to help us, comfort us, direct us, educate us, and change us. You are a good God.*

Unfortunately, the lie didn't just "poof" and go away. It took me some time to process and let the truth sink in. I needed time with the Lord, needed to hear Him and understand and believe the truth that He offered. After getting the kids settled the next night, I snuck away to soak in the tub, went back over the Scriptures, and started to see the light. I was in the tub, shaking my head again in disbelief. Was this truth? Can my husband be trusted?

After my soak, I slowly and bravely went downstairs and sat across the room from him. I felt so vulnerable and so raw. I asked him if we could talk, pouring my heart out and revealing how I had been feeling for the entire twelve years of our marriage. I was ROBBED! For twelve years, I lived with the thought that if I didn't do more or better, my husband would find someone else. I talked at length with him that night. We discussed marriage, our love for each other, and so much more that needed to be said. After an hour of deep and heavy discussion, during which my husband had to defend himself and prove I was wrong in my thinking, he said something that stuck. He said, "I don't deserve the blame you put on me when you look at how I have treated you and how I have honored you since BEFORE we were even married." And he was right. He didn't deserve the accusations and the pit I had put him in, waiting for him to cheat.

Something in me changed that night, and I stopped obsessing over the idea of him cheating on me. It wasn't instant, but I took control of my thoughts. The lie that would come to my mind and cause me to worry, doubt, and fear had to be stopped in its tracks when it came in. I accepted I was the woman he chose and would choose again. It didn't happen overnight, but I felt some relief, referring to the Scripture my friends shared from Philippians, encouraging me to focus on the truth and the praiseworthy. I also remembered my husband's statement that he didn't deserve this accusation, and I trusted in God and in him. I also stood on our commitment to each other and to God from the day we married.

We demolish arguments and every pretension that sets
*itself up against the knowledge of God, and we **take***
***captive every thought** to make it obedient to Christ.*
2 CORINTHIANS 10:5 NIV, EMPHASIS ADDED

To escape the lie, I had to capture that lie and take captive every thought to be free! Whenever accusations crept in, I would stop and ask myself, "Is it true? Is this the character of my husband? Has he done anything or said anything to prove himself untrustworthy?" The answer was always, "Not even close!"

Freedom and peace came as I attacked and held captive those lies and dismissed them. Scripture is so powerful! I couldn't have overcome this on my own. The work of the Holy Spirit led me to the truth, and it was Jesus who fought that battle for me.

If you have experienced this freedom, it is indescribable. Jesus has done that for us, and we have to claim it. Don't let it go to waste. He didn't die for us and win the battle against the devil (who, by the way, is the father of lies) for nothing. No, dig in and get to the truth. Drop those lies that ensnare you! Digging deep and getting to the root of our insecurities, pain, and lies is worth the pain. Let Him heal you like He healed me. He gave me the freedom I didn't even know I could have, and He can do the same for you.

HONEY NUGGET

When we surrender our deepest fears to
Jesus and let His truth replace the lies, the
prison doors swing open, and we step into
a freedom and peace only He can give.

CHAPTER 21

SEARCHING FOR DIAMONDS

For my thirty-seventh birthday, my husband gave me a beautiful pair of diamond earrings, which I wore every single day. I love those diamonds so much. They were not only beautiful but also precious to me because they were a gift from him. Well, I lost them and panicked when I couldn't find them. How could I do this? I was so careful, but was I? I did not want to have to tell my husband I lost them—not yet, anyway. So I made it my mission to find them. I searched high and low in every drawer in the bathroom and on the floor around my nightstand, thinking they had to be in the house because I lost both, not just one. I was frantically moving around, thinking how horrible and foolish I was to misplace them. It was not like me at all to misplace those earrings since I always took them off at night and put them in my jewelry dish. After hours of searching, I was hot and sweaty and at my wit's end. Then it occurred to me that God knows everything, so maybe I should ask Him for help.

I was crouching down in my bathroom on my two feet with knees bent so I was kind of like a ball. I couldn't even stand up because I was at a loss. I had just looked through all my bathroom drawers and had no idea where I should go next. From that position, I prayed:

> *Lord Jesus, You know where my earrings are. Would You*
> *please remind me where they are? I am desperate. I am sorry*
> *I didn't ask You until now.*

Right beside me was the bottom drawer where I kept all the back stock items, like toilet paper, tissues, and my travel bags for all of my toiletries. It was like I was a robot. I pulled the drawer open, grabbed a travel bag, and unzipped it. There were the sparkling, shining diamonds. I had put them in there when I had gone for a girls' day at the spa and did not remember putting them safely inside so I wouldn't lose them. I am pretty sure I am not alone in this. Have you ever put something precious in a safe spot and then you couldn't remember the safe spot? It was just a little too safe!

> *Are You kidding me, Lord? Access to You is abundant. You*
> *knew. You revealed the answer immediately.*

Yet again, I did my own thing running around like a chicken with my head cut off, trying to solve my problems when Jesus, Prince of Peace, the all-knowing King of the universe, was accessible and available to me. Jesus said to the disciples before He left earth that He would send a Helper—the Holy Spirit.

> *And I will pray to the Father, and He will give you*
> *another Helper, that He may abide with you forever—the*

Spirit of truth, whom the world cannot receive, because
it neither sees Him nor knows Him; but you know
Him, for He dwells with you and will be in you.
JOHN 14:16-17 NIV

So let me ask—do you pray to Him, talk with Him, and seek Him? You have full access to the Holy Spirit, who listens, speaks, and responds. He is our Helper as we navigate life—the good and the bad, the storms and the calm, the highs and the lows. What a gift from God! Jesus Himself asked the Father to send the Holy Spirit to be with us, and that changes everything. Because Jesus came, we are not only forgiven, but we also have the privilege of walking with the Spirit every single day.

HONEY NUGGET

God delights in guiding us, not just through storms
but also in the everyday details of our lives.

CHAPTER 22

YELLOW BUTTERFLIES

I had this very skewed and morbid idea that when my kids went away to college, it was as if they were dying. It was the strangest thing. Like the day they left, it would be all over. I would suddenly not be a mom anymore, and poof, they would disappear. As we all know, that is not the case. But they did fly the coop, and my role as a mom, which I had been doing for eighteen years, changed and morphed into a different role. This wasn't a new thing; it had been a fluid change since they were born and as they grew and matured. My role had new responsibilities and purposes with each new age and stage. I could see that I was working myself out of my favorite job in the world, and that was where my irrational but very real "poof, the kids will disappear" fear was born.

Were there setbacks on the journey of raising children? Of course, there were many! But our overall goal was to grow, nurture, and point our kids to Jesus so that someday they could do it on their own. Reaching their hearts and showing them Jesus was the goal and our biggest priority. That idea seems so refined, easy, and elegant. As anyone who has ever cared for a child knows, it is not easy. There were so many hard days. I remember back to the first night in the hospital when Jake was born. I was panicked and stressed. I was so overwhelmed that I didn't sleep at all, feeling I had the weight of the world on me like I had never felt before. How in the world did my mom do this five times?

I took this new role as a mom very seriously and probably a little too extreme. Over time, I was the stereotypical, so-called "crazy" new mom who watched my child sleep and had charts for all his feedings and dirty diapers. I was fanatical about his schedule and doing all the right things: reading books, calling friends, and probably spending too much time at the pediatrician. I pretty much forgot to feed myself in the first few months as well. I was exhausted and felt like I couldn't do enough, like nobody told me what motherhood was really like. I joined the mom club, but somehow, the contract details were hidden until he was born. Then, bam—here is your little bundle—go figure it out!

It took me some time to calm down and not freak out over every little thing. Jake was a delight, and I have said a million times, "Oh, the poor firstborn." They are definitely the guinea pigs. Remember, I said I always wanted to be a mom, so it was my pleasure to figure this mom job out and do it to the best of my ability. I loved every moment—after I calmed myself down, of course.

Fast forward eighteen years, it was 2018, and my firstborn was a college freshman. He attended Chapman University in Orange County, California, which was about ninety minutes from our home in San Diego. I missed him so much and tried not to call or text him too much so he wouldn't be annoyed with me. But since the day I found out I was pregnant with him, I fell in love with him. Now he was gone; again, not forever, but it sure felt like it!

You can imagine my sheer elation when he called me one fall day asking for a few items from his bedroom that he needed and wondered if I had any time that week to drive them up to him. I had zero hesitation about going immediately! Within twenty minutes, I was flying up Interstate 5! Picture the windows down, the music blaring, and a mom on a mission! I mean, I couldn't get there fast enough. He invited me to his school, so, of course, I said, "YES!"

I arrived at his dorm parking lot and felt like I was a kid going to Disneyland. The anticipation of seeing Jake was growing and only moments away. I texted him and waited for him. As he walked out of his building and toward my parked car, I saw a young man who was dressed in a collared shirt with every little hair on his head in place. He looked so handsome, so grown up, so independent. My eyes witnessed the fruit of all those years of sowing. All those crazy mornings before school, "Where's your backpack? Do you have your lunch? Hurry, we are going to be late! Get in the car!" flashed in my mind. All those years, and now he was doing it all on his own. Then my mind flashed back to when he was two and running around and so happy with life! He was a joy and, yes, a pile of work, but my joy. How was he in college? How did eighteen years fly by so fast?

Lord, thank You for Jake.

We hugged hello, I gave him the items, had a short conversation, and then I hugged him again so tightly. I hadn't thought about having to say goodbye because I was so focused on getting there. I saw him for no more than five minutes, and he had to go drop the items in his dorm and get to class.

AHHHH! No, I just got here. I have so much to say to you! I love you; I want more time with you. No, you are mine. No, you aren't. You are the Lord's, and you have to go to school. I have so many questions: How is school, and how are your roommates? How is the laundry detergent working, and are you changing your sheets?

However, I had to say goodbye. I hugged his tall, thin frame and kissed the side of his neck. That is my signature move where I kiss all of my boys. The side of their neck is just where I can reach on my tiptoes, and a hug is just not sufficient for me. The kiss seals it for me. Every single time. I wonder if they even realize that I have made this my signature move? My relationship with each of my boys is special and unique. I didn't want to let go, but I did. I held it together until he walked away as I didn't want him to know I was upset. That wouldn't be fair to put my heartache on him. He was fine! He was loving school and thriving.

As I watched him walk back to his dorm, everything was in slow motion, and it felt like my body was five hundred pounds as I tried to pull my legs through the quicksand toward the driver's side of the car. My arms could barely lift the handle open to get in the car. I was struggling, and my brain and my body were barely cooperating. Oh, my heart! It was breaking again. I still feel that familiar pain in my chest even now as I write this. It is the same pain I had driving away from my preemie Ryan still in the hospital. The same pain I had to go through three times driving away after we dropped each boy off at college for the first time. The same pain when my dear mother-in-law passed away to heaven. I guess that is why it is called heartbreak. It is the worst because it hurts so much.

I was unsafe to drive at that point because I was hysterical, so I paused to compose myself. I looked up at the building where I could see his room on the top floor. There was a tall eucalyptus tree that reached his window on the third floor. Tears streaming down my face, I began to pray.

> *Dear Lord, be with him, and thank You for him. These eighteen years went so fast, but I know You have great plans for him to prosper and grow. This is his time You have planned for him to be at college. It is not about me. He is Yours. I love him so much, but You love him more. You love him perfectly. You are with him even though I can't be. Lord, help me. This hurts so bad.*

While I cried out to the Lord, my mind shifted. I stopped and looked back at Jake's dorm window and the towering eucalyptus trees, imagining him getting to his room to drop off the items and grab his backpack for school. And then I saw it. There were hundreds of yellow butterflies fluttering and dancing in the warm, fall Santa Ana breeze around the tree next to his window. I had an idea! Every time I saw a yellow butterfly, I would pray for him.

> *Lord, You are with him and can see him at all times. You know what he needs and can send Your Holy Spirit.*

It was something I could do from afar, not knowing where Jake was, but the Lord did.

> *And the Lord, He is the One who goes before you. He will be with you, He will not leave you nor forsake you; do not fear nor be dismayed.*
>
> DEUTERONOMY 31:8

I will be with you. I will not leave you nor forsake you.
JOSHUA 1:5

Do not be afraid, nor dismayed, for the Lord
your God is with you wherever you go.
JOSHUA 1:9

The only way I was able to drive away from Jake was knowing how much the Lord loved him and how He would never leave him. This was about me letting go of my deep desire to hold on to Jake with everything I had. I had to surrender him to the Lord and trust Him with the purpose He made Jake for. It was imperative I make this shift so I would not be the weird mom in the parking lot who stayed overnight. Over and over, I said in my mind, "The Lord loves him more than I do. He will never leave him. He has great plans for Jake."

I had to believe this was not about me. I had to take the focus off of myself and what I wanted. The words of Pastor Rick Warren came to my mind, "It's not about you. The purpose of your life is far greater than your own personal fulfillment, your peace of mind, or even your happiness. It's far greater than your family, your career, or even your wildest dreams and ambitions."[8] I had to believe not just for me but for Jake, as well.

I began to see yellow butterflies everywhere I went. I would say a prayer for Jake each time, prompted by the Holy Spirit. Very quickly, I assigned the other two of my boys a butterfly color: white butterflies for Ryan and all other butterfly colors for Luke. I am one busy mom praying for my boys throughout my day. I love it as I don't feel abandoned or like I lost my job as a mom. I still have a job; it just looks different. I am just as active and trusting the Lord with my most precious people that the Lord has entrusted us to grow into godly men. I have to smile when I see a butterfly fly across a busy traffic intersection or on a walk on the beach.

HONEY NUGGET

When we release our children into God's hands, we discover that His presence is the safest place they could ever be.

CHAPTER 23

MOVE TO TEXAS

As I write the stories that have shaped my life, I'm struck by how many mistakes I can now see in hindsight. It was those mistakes and hardships that have formed my view of life and of God. Looking back is both humbling and exhilarating as I trace the threads of His presence, realizing that even when I was unaware of His work, His love, and His plans, He was there. He has been with me all along. They also give me encouragement for my future and all of the unknowns that lie ahead.

Up until now in all of my stories I have seen the Lord at work, and they ALL work out—husband found, babies were born, prayers were answered. But this story is about the unfolding and trusting of the Lord when I still can't see how it will turn out. The comfortable things in life are no problem. Mountaintops are glorious, fun, and spectacular! The uncomfortable, the unknown, the unanswered parts of life that make you stop and question everything—not so much fun.

I am trusting the Lord with my life and my family's life. We moved to Dallas from San Diego in November 2021. We left behind a city that I grew up in, went to school in, found my husband in, had my kids in, and raised them in. This may sound like an amazing adventure to you, but for me and the way God made me, it was challenging and took me some time to get on board with.

So my Mr. More-Than-I-Could-Think-Or-Imagine husband is a visionary. He loves adventure and travel, seeing life so differently than I do. Which I love. I love that we both bring our own uniqueness to the table because it means our life is fuller and more complete. If I made all of the decisions in our lives, I would be home most of the day, perhaps meet a friend for lunch or stroll through the mall, and then head straight back home again. I am a homebody for sure. He, on the other hand, can't sit still and has to be going, doing, producing, building, at all times. We usually meet in the middle and stretch each other out of our comfort zones, which is so good for us to grow.

This is the third time we have made a big move in our married life. Every time I am heartbroken and hate the thought of going somewhere new. Then God does something huge in my heart, and I learn that He is trustworthy. So by this third move (the first was Kona, Hawaii, and the second was London, England), you would have thought I would have been so good and used to leaving my home in San Diego. But this time was different. This time we were buying a house and making a permanent move. Michael and his team had researched, visited, and considered four different places to move the headquarters of the company and ultimately chose Dallas, Texas, for many reasons. Michael wanted to have the headquarters of the growing business in a more affordable place for the hundreds of employees of MD7 to live and work. It was also more centrally located to his customers. His European customers and offices were also that much closer to Texas compared to California. It made perfect sense to me logically, but it still was hard to swallow. We would have to say goodbye to everything we knew and move it all.

I was in the exact same spot trying to convince him that we shouldn't move. This was a major move for us, and it felt very permanent. I tried to share my heart and all the reasons I didn't want to move. I complained to him and to all our friends. It was causing a rift in our usually loving and perfectly calm, sweet marriage.

I told Michael, "Of course I am going to go with you because you are my husband and I will follow you anywhere you go. But I really need confirmation from the Lord. I have been expecting to hear from Him, and I am still waiting." Michael understood and continued to coordinate moving the company. I knew God was good but wondered how in the world He was going to pull this off. I was reminded, again, that He is always available. I need to lean in and search for Him.

You will seek Me and find Me, when you
search for Me with all your heart.
JEREMIAH 29:13

I told the Lord I wanted Him to give me Scripture that we were supposed to move. I wanted Scripture from the Lord's mouth, His Word. I told the Lord how I felt and basically lamented my fears, worries, and sadness on Him. He heard every detail of what my heart was feeling. I prayed and searched God's Word and was waiting for confirmation for months. In my Bible, I wrote dates and little notes to remind me of what was going on in my life. My Bible is a plethora of notes, names, stories, dates, etc. I do it so I can remember what

God said so I can stand on His truth. Notice that all of my notes about moving have a little sad face next to them.

My soul melts from heaviness; strengthen
me according to Your word.
PSALM 119:28

:(

10/29/20

I would have lost heart, unless I had believed that I would
see the goodness of the Lord in the land of the living.
PSALM 27:13

:(

10/21/20

Hear my cry, O God; attend to my prayer. From the
end of the earth I will cry to You., when my heart is
overwhelmed; lead me to the rock that is higher than I.
PSALM 61:1-2

:(

11/20/20

I had two reasons why I didn't want to leave San Diego. First, I didn't want our G5 family to be broken up and the boys not have a "home" to come back to. I knew wives and grandbabies would come after some time, and I wanted more than anything to be with the grandkids while they grew up. And secondly, I didn't want to be away from my K19 family. My mom and dad are getting older, and my dad is pretty sick with Parkinson's disease. He was a big, tough marine, and now this debilitating disease is taking its toll on his body. I just wanted to stay close by to help and be available.

The Lord knew my heart, and I desperately needed Him. When two of my sweet, long-time friends, Hallie and Suzy and I would meet for our weekly coffee and catch-up, I would ask them for prayer for direction and peace. I wanted Scripture that I could turn to anytime it got hard, like those nights when I would wake up in the dark of the night and feel totally alone and so far away from what I knew. For those days when it was hard to get up and get my day started because I was missing my family so badly. The most precious thing in the whole world is God's direction and encouragement so I asked and waited—and read—and searched. It had been months of quiet times with the Lord. I was desperate to hear from the Lord, expecting to hear from Him. I was seeking like I never had before!

> *As a deer pants for streams of water, so*
> *my soul pants for you, my God.*
> PSALM 42:1 NIV

It was 12/21/2020 when I received the Scripture that I had been waiting for. When the Lord spoke with the Holy Spirit to me about our move. I cannot properly articulate the words or the flood of security and peace that I felt. Part of what I felt was so loved, so heard, and so understood. I mean, SO LOVED, SO HEARD, AND SO UNDERSTOOD! This is the sole purpose in sharing my story with you so you too can KNOW HIM and HAVE A RELATIONSHIP WITH HIM, EXPERIENCING THE GOODNESS OF HIM. It's like the best hug of reassurance and love. This is what I had with Him.

> *However, when He, the Spirit of truth has*
> *come, He will guide you into all truth.*
> JOHN 16:13

Dane Ortlund describes the encounter with the Lord so beautifully. In *Gentle and Lowly* Ortlund states that "the Spirit makes the heart of Christ real to us; not just heard, but seen, not just seen, but felt; not just felt, but enjoyed."[9] Ortlund continues to give the analogy of a small child being told he is loved by his father. The child believes him and takes his word, "but, it is another thing, unutterably more real, to be swept up in his embrace, to feel the warmth, to hear his beating heart within his chest, to instantly know the protective grip of his arms. It's one thing to hear he loves you; it's another thing to feel his love. This is the glorious work of the Spirit."[10]

I am sitting in a coffee shop with tears so big welling in my eyes I can barely see what I am writing. He is right here with us waiting for us to talk to Him to seek Him. So I finally got the Scripture that said, "Heidi, move to Texas, I have got you. I have got great plans for you, your sons, and your grandchildren." I had the peace that was surpassing my understanding. I was content with God's encouragement and leading. Here is the Scripture that leapt off the page and pierced my heart with a love arrow.

> *Now this is the commandment, and these are the statutes*
> *and judgments which the Lord your God has commanded*
> *to teach you, that you may observe them in the land which*
> *you are crossing over to possess, that you may fear the Lord*
> *your God, to keep all His statutes and His commandments*
> *which I command you, you and your son and your*
> *grandson, all the days of your life, and that your days may*

be prolonged. Therefore hear, O Israel, and be careful to
observe it, that it may be well with you, and that you
may multiply greatly as the Lord God of your fathers has
promised you—"a land flowing with milk and honey."
DEUTERONOMY 6:1-4

:)

That was it. I read and reread it and dove into the meaning of every word. God spoke straight to my soul and my deepest concerns. Doesn't He always do this for us? I love how He ALWAYS knows what is best. I love that He is trustworthy. I underlined two parts in that Scripture. First, "That you may observe them in the land which you are crossing over to possess," and second, "That you may fear the Lord your God, to keep all the statutes and His commandments which I command you and your son and your grandsons." I love Him so much. He was talking about moving over to Texas from California. And for me, I had never read about grandchildren in the Bible, so when I read this about my sons and their children, I knew it was for me. That was one of my biggest concerns for our G5 family. I was reassured He has a plan and He knows! Please notice the smiley face after the Scripture.

The other part that satisfied my fear was that we were able to keep our forever San Diego home. We would be able to fly back if my parents needed me and have a place to stay. That assurance meant so much to me. Do you want to hear the other incredible part that there is no way we could have orchestrated all the parts into a fabulous story without God? Do you know where two of my three sons went to school? In Texas! Are you kidding me? Luke chose Southern Methodist University, SMU, well before we decided to move, and I promise we did not follow him. Ryan had wanted to go to Baylor in

Waco, Texas, since he was eight years old when RG3 (professional football player) was a superstar there, so when he received his acceptance letter, it was for sure a yes. And Jake stayed in our San Diego home and finished his last two years at the University of San Diego, USD. Do you know what that meant? It meant that both our homes were somewhat close to our boys.

The other part of Scripture that intrigued me was "a land flowing with milk and honey." It reminded me of *Willy Wonka and the Chocolate Factory* by Roald Dahl with the stream of chocolate and the candy trees and bushes and everything was made of sweets. I mean, that was forever embedded in my brain as a child, maybe you too. So when I read, "A land flowing with milk and honey," I had to know more. My mind saw a beautiful land with rivers and streams with protein-packed and super-nourishing white milk, with honey dripping from the beehives that were hanging from the trees. The land was the most beautiful, vibrant, fertile land. There were all kinds of colorful flowers and trees, really almost fake it was so perfect. There were horses and cows, dogs and cats, butterflies and honeybees happily flying around (no creepy critters and especially no roaches).

So next, I did a deep dive on what God meant by this and was so excited to learn again what a gracious and good God we have. The story in Deuteronomy is telling of how the Israelites have been in bondage and slavery and how the Lord has rescued them from their deep despair. They were free, and not just free but given a whole new abundant life. We are just like the Israelites. Before we "know" Christ and accept Him as our Savior, we are living in sin and bondage, many times not even knowing we are living in a prison cell. But with this free gift of forgiving our sins, we are not only set free but also offered an abundant life here and now and forever! We are invited to step out of the prison cell and live a whole new, free life of abundance. This is so exciting! We don't have to wait to die and go to heaven someday to enjoy the abundant life. No, God is with us now, and we have the free gift of abundant life here and now.

Pastor Jon Courson explains in his *Application Commentary Old Testament, Volume 1* "Milk is a staple. Honey is a luxury. Milk gives you strength. Honey is sweet. God says, 'I want to bring you into the land of milk and honey—the place of strength and sweetness. How does that happen? Listen to me and it will go well with you.'"[11] I hope these stories I have shared will encourage you to look at your life and see God's goodness, His abundant life of milk and honey, what we need and what is an extra blessing or luxury all over you and your life!

What is the beauty of us moving away from these precious people? The gift is we are able to return to San Diego and we make every moment count. We see our people more than when we lived there because we know our time is limited. At this time, we are living with everything we need and the extra blessing and luxury that I see is the sweet time we get to see our family and friends when we go back to San Diego for a visit. It is just so sweet, the honey of my life. I am grateful. God is so generous in His care and attention to every detail.

HONEY NUGGET

The same God who calls us to leave what is familiar is the One who goes before us, carrying both our fears and our future in His hands.

CHAPTER 24

FREEDOM FROM LIES: MY FREQUENT FLIER

Remember that first lie I had about Michael cheating on me? My second lie that wiggled its way into my head, which had been there since I was at least five years old, was that husbands and dads travel to get away from their wives and kids to have a break and be with their friends. I know it sounds absurd, and if you laughed out loud, I would not be surprised. My hardworking dad was a very successful salesman and traveled quite a bit to visit customers. He worked long hours, and I would miss him most mornings and evenings as he worked crazy hours to provide for our family. These absent days and hours affected my young heart, making me feel unworthy of him or his love. He had more important things to do than spend time with me.

Now, I understand this was a selfish way of looking at his hardworking character. Still, nonetheless, the lie that was attached to me was I was not worth enough for him to stay home or spend quality time with me.

Fast forward to marrying my travel-loving husband who worked his tail off and traveled all the time. Ouch. You see my pain, don't you? I never put up a fight when he would leave on yet another trip, but I was not happy about it. I was distant and quiet and became so annoyed with yet another trip he would be planning. I knew this was wrong and that I was acting so childishly. If I tried to talk to him about it, I would get totally crushed. "You want me to stay home and not work?" It sounded absolutely crazy. I tried to change him and his schedule, but what I needed to change was me. This lie attached itself to me because I thought this was the truth. I would have physical manifestations due to this worry and the anxiety it put on me at the mere mention that another trip was coming.

Then I looked to God for help and reflected on myself to figure out how it happened, but even better, how to get rid of this lie. I named it my freedom from the frequent flier lie. It is fun to name these lies and laugh about them once I release them when I am finally free! This is how I got my freedom after having been caged for more than forty years.

It was October, and my husband's birthday was coming up when he said he was going to Austin with the guys for five days to watch the Formula One race. Ouchhhhhh! All I heard him say was, "You are not fun enough for me to stay home with you! You are boring, Heidi. You are not worth it. These guys are so much better than you! He is staying five days to maximize his time away to get the much-needed break away from you! He is happier without you!" Are you laughing or crying over those statements?

After he left for work, I crawled back into bed and cried. I ugly cried to the point that I had snot all over my pillow and my head hurt from all the tears of anguish. I did not know what to do with myself; the lies just kept coming over and over in my head about how unworthy and unlovable I was. After I could not cry another tear, I decided to go to the Lord and get help. I had exhausted all my options to make him stay, and sadly, after I figured out I couldn't fix this on my own, I went to the Lord EXPECTING help.

So I staggered out of my snot- and tear-drenched bed and went to my desk with my Bible and my notebook. I started talking to God and wrote down EVERYTHING I was thinking and feeling. Tears continued to roll down my face as I wrote it all out. I paused and listened, desperately seeking direction, wisdom, or comfort from the Lord. Literally, I wrestled with the Lord to get my freedom from this. I knew God was powerful and able, and I was adamant that I would find an answer from Him. After writing for a while, I went to my Jon Courson *Application Commentary* set. There are three volumes of commentaries in which he explains Scripture verse by verse. I love them so much because I love to read Jon's book when I want clarity or more knowledge or wisdom on a specific Scripture. It is the same commentary as the one I was reading in London at the window seat.

I looked at the table of contents where he lists small stories that go with some of the Scripture and saw one titled, "Let Glow of Your Issues." To be honest, I was searching for "How Do You Get Your Husband to not Go on a Trip." Just kidding. I knew it would not be that easy, but I hoped it would be that clear. I kept reading the titles in the table of contents and then was urged to return to the glow story. Weird. Glow? However, I believe that the Holy Spirit was pointing me to that story. I could not figure out why it would help, but I decided to read it if the Lord was leading me to it. I looked like crap from all the tears, so sure, give me some glow.

As I began to read this story, I was looking for an answer, and then it came! I am still in awe, and I still get chills and tears in my eyes when I talk about how the Lord spoke to me. The Lord, the God of the universe, pointed me to the story that led to my freedom from the lies of the frequent flier that I had believed to be true for more than forty years. I had been hostage to this lie, and for twenty-four years of my marriage and for all of my childhood that I can remember, I believed that the most important men in my life would leave. They didn't leave me; they left to work (or play), and it was not a reflection of me but rather life. It is so interesting how a normal event in life—a dad leaving for work or a husband going on a guys' trip— would put me spinning and in a deep world of hurt.

The story that Jon Courson used for the illustration was about a woman who had been bleeding for twelve years and was frantically searching for an answer to stop her bleeding. I was doing the same things, frantically trying to stop my husband from traveling. She had alienated herself from everyone because she was so obnoxious while looking for the answer. I was obnoxious as well. On the outside I looked and acted fine, but inside my head was a horrible storm! It was out of control. Jesus was her answer, and He was mine. She touched the hem of His cloak, and with that one touch her bleeding stopped.[12] My favorite fabric swatch in my desk drawer had gone out of stock. It was white with dark gray, little, unsymmetrical circles, and its edge was fringed. It was perfect.

So I prayed and talked to God and claimed this in my heart and life. Jesus was my answer, and I could be healed of this lie in "one touch." And I was. I hung the fabric swatch on my pencil holder to see it and be reminded of God's faithfulness in healing me from this lie. The Lord is so loving, kind, and gentle. I was exhausted from the hours I had spent with the Lord digging and revealing the deepest parts of my soul. I felt good but tired.

A few weeks later, the big trip came, and I said goodbye. I was fine, waiting for an avalanche of lies to enter my mind, but it was quiet. I decided to make a new note on my phone during those five days that listed all the things I saw show up from God and titled it GG (God's Good). He was with me. I was not alone, and I would make the best of these days and watch the Lord show up. I had the best time, all the while claiming the promise of the Lord on my life and my new freedom. I am free and no longer shrink into my head when Michael says he is leaving. Instead, I am free, and it is all because of the power of Jesus. It took one touch after I chose to seek Him.

He forgives all my sins. He heals me.
PSALM 103:3 TLB

He healed me, and I am so free. Any time my husband says he is leaving on another trip, I feel calm and peaceful. Yes, I miss him, but I am fine! Praise the Lord, for He is so good to me and to you. I urge you to seek Him, hear the truth, trust Him, and touch His garment. The freedom from fear and worry is indescribable.

HONEY NUGGET

Even the deepest, oldest lies lose their grip when we reach for Jesus. One touch from Him can bring a lifetime of freedom and peace.

CHAPTER 25

THE AIRPORT, DIANA, AND CHICK-N-MINIS®

Whenever I have an early flight out of Dallas Love Field airport, I get Chick-fil-A Chick-n-Minis® for breakfast. The minis are small, bite-sized chicken nuggets wrapped in warm honey-basted biscuits that melt in your mouth. If you know, you know; if you don't, I suggest you try them. You will not regret it. They are glorious, and the small reward I get for peeling myself out of my favorite place in the world—my bed—to make it to the airport on time. Plus, I don't get the minis outside of the airport. That is what makes traveling so exciting. The sweet anticipation for the next time I get to reward myself.

I like having little things that keep me motivated and disciplined. So when we arrive at the airport, we head straight to Chick-fil-A. The line is always long. And by long, I mean Disney lines long. This morning was no different. The line of hungry travelers snaked back and forth and stretched down half the terminal, past the Hudson Newsstand and a kiosk that sold T-shirts that claimed *Everything is Bigger in Texas*. But the minis are non-negotiable, and I had to have them. I didn't care how long the line was; I was willing to wait with patience and determination.

While I spent upwards of an hour with the people in line, I became "friends" with a woman in front of me and the man behind me. The woman was in her forties, and by the way she restlessly moved from one foot to the other, shifting her weight and placing her hands on hips, I could tell she was lacking in the patience and determination department. After the first thirty minutes of looking at the back of the woman's head, she turned around to make sure the rest of the line knew that she was not happy to be at (what I considered) the true happiest place on earth. She let us all know that she was begrudgingly in line to get her ungrateful teen daughter food. She "hated" Chick-fil-A as an organization and couldn't understand why her daughter insisted on this food and couldn't believe she was standing in that line waiting that long for "this kind of food." The woman said if she had a spray can, she would spray obscenities across the front counter. Wow! Okay. So "friends" was a bit of an exaggeration. I downgraded our budding relationship to line partners, at best.

I said a quick prayer to the Lord to help love her and listen to her. She was struggling in life and shared some pretty intimate details about her life struggles. The woman admitted that she had been hurt by the "church" and by people, and now she was bitter and angry. Rightly so, it is unfortunate when people are hurt in the one place they go for healing and they assign that hurt to God. He is the innocent bystander who is blamed and accused; because of this, people will pull away from Him. She clearly had been traumatized in the church she attended by people who needed Jesus just as much as she did, and because of that, she was criticizing the business because she knew Chick-fil-A and the church had similar beliefs.

I never caught her name, but I tried to validate her feelings and empathize with her while simultaneously asking Jesus for words to say and questions to ask.

> *Jesus, what do I say to this woman? Help me to love her as*
> *You do and ask the right questions to point her to You.*

Conveniently (though we all know God placed me exactly where I was at that very moment), I was sandwiched between her and a man named Christian who worked for an airline and was on a break. Christian was an older, clean-cut man who wore a Southwest Airlines uniform. He said he worked "underneath the terminal" and that there are many moving parts to make our flights happen. We quickly jumped topics to the Lord and His goodness. It was easy to see that he loved the Lord, and by the time we were done talking, I knew he knew I did too.

At the same time, my husband, Michael, was waiting at our gate, nervous we would miss our flight. He texted me that he was going to leave the gate and see if another food vendor would be faster. But there was no way I was giving up my spot in line. I had to have my Chick-n-Minis®! It was tradition and a bit of an obsession. I texted Michael, assuring him I would make it to the front in time and urging him to come back and join me in line to experience the mayhem of hungry travelers. But oh, the pressure I felt when he walked back, and I still had thirty people in front of me.

Please, Lord, I have another small and silly request: Can You help us get food for our flight, particularly the Chick-n-Minis®?

I have another beautiful story of why these minis mean so much to me and why I was willing to wait for so long for them that particular morning. Not only do those little bites of perfection taste delicious, but they hold a very special meaning to me. They are God's little way of saying, "I see you, Heidi, and you are not alone. I am with you." Just thinking about them makes tears well up in my eyes. The first time I had a Chick-n-Mini®, Michael and I were on our first trip to see his very sick mom, Diana, in Palm Desert, California. She was unexpectedly hospitalized due to an insane infection in her body that quickly turned to sepsis. Within no time she was on life support. We were obviously in a rush to get to her and be by her side. It was before that early morning flight when I discovered the Chick-n-Minis® in the airport.

As Michael and I ate our food in silence that dark and scary morning, I prayed to Jesus to help us. I felt like a little girl having to take on a big girl job, and I wasn't ready.

Jesus, what do I do? What do I say? How do I handle this?

I again said, almost out loud, I didn't feel ready or qualified to take on the unknown and was scared of what we were going to find once we reached the hospital. As I talked to God, I told Him I didn't think I could do this.

I don't want to do this, Jesus. This is too hard.

As I slowly forced myself to eat my newly discovered minis, Jesus assured me that He saw me and loved me and that Michael and I were not alone. After a long, deep breath and a newly found confidence that I was certain was courtesy of the Holy Spirit, I knew that with Jesus I could and would be able to handle whatever we found.

It was this morning when I started to associate God's comfort with the minis. That little box of warm goodness provided a sense of comfort and reassurance, just like the presence of a caring friend. Each bite felt like a consoling embrace during challenging times, reminding me that I was not alone and that there was always hope.

Michael and I were walking into the uncomfortable and the unknown. From the night we shared our vows and recited "for better for worse," we knew there would be a day when we faced "for worse," just like the night our miracle baby Ryan was born. As we stepped into the hospital after arriving by airplane, we knew that this was the day and we were about to walk into really hard things. My heart hurt like Michael's heart hurt. We were one, not only with each other but also with Jesus. We were in this together.

Seeing someone you love in such a helpless state is so hard. When we got to the ICU, we literally walked right by her lying in her bed. We didn't know it was her; she was unrecognizable. The doctors explained the severity of the situation. It was heart-wrenching because the pain of seeing her suffer those last weeks was close to unbearable; that is the bitter part.

But Jesus was with us. I had my eyes wide open, looking for Him as we tackled each day, sitting by her side for hours on end, even though she could not interact with us.

I will say of the Lord, "He is my refuge and my fortress;
my God, in Him I will trust.

PSALM 91:2

Even there, Your hand shall lead me,
and Your right hand shall hold me.
PSALM 139:10

But I will sing of Your power; Yes, I will sing aloud of Your
mercy in the morning; for you have been my defense and
refuge in the day of my trouble. To You, O my Strength, I
will sing praises; for God is my defense, my God of Mercy.
PSALM 59:16-17 EMPHASIS ADDED

We felt so much pain for her, and it broke our hearts that we couldn't take it away. We held her hand and talked with her. But the joy of knowing she is now made new again and in heaven softens the pain in my heart even today. I will see her again. I will laugh with her again as she was among the funniest ladies I knew. That time with her was so painful; it was difficult to even form words into sentences, out loud or in my head. I repeated over and over:

Jesus. Jesus. Jesus.

Thankfully, He knew my thoughts and would fill in where I needed it. And He did. Jesus was the bit of honey, the hope, the goodness in our hard situation. After multiple early morning trips over the next two weeks, we unfortunately lost Michael's mother, Diana. She was now in heaven after weeks of fighting a severe infection in her body. I imagine her playing tennis and loving her new body, reuniting with loved ones and, most importantly, being in the presence of the Lord! He is the sweet, good, and worthy part that gives me hope. Those minis were tangible reminders to me that God is near. He is my strength. He is my comfort.

So now you can understand why waiting forty-five minutes was worth every moment to me to get those Chick-N-Minis®. The lady graciously offered to let me go in front of her so I could make my flight to be a bit closer to the front. I had finally reached the cashier.

Thank you, Lord!

By that time, Michael had already left *AND* boarded the plane. With a smile that was beginning to strain my cheeks and the enthusiasm of a Texas cheerleader performing under the Friday night lights, I ordered his sandwich and my minis. My sheer delight turned to defeat when I heard the worker say, "Sorry, ma'am, no minis; we are out." It was as if the entire terminal began to spin in slow motion around me as I stood completely still and in shock. I had no words. I turned around and looked at the woman, who was now directly behind me, and Christian, the airline worker, whom I had by then convinced with my incessant praise and extreme detail about how delicious they were to order *THE MINIS!* They both stared back at me with wide-eyed shared disbelief. I know they felt my pain. I had no choice but to quickly order something else and *RUN* to my flight. I took the food bag, turned, and said goodbye to them. Christian and I exchanged a heartfelt "God bless you," and I sprinted to the plane.

After boarding, I settled into my seat across the aisle from Michael. I was still shocked that I made the flight with food, but more importantly, I couldn't believe they ran out of my sought after minis. I stowed my overly packed bag under the seat in front of me. I was bent down to get my iPad and AirPods and missed the entire interaction that took place next.

Christian, the airline worker and my line buddy, made his way down the aisle of the plane. When he reached our row, he stopped and with a beaming smile handed my husband a box of hot minis and said, "These are for your wife. They discovered one last order right after she left. So I found your plane and want to give them to her." I sat up in my seat as I watched him walk away, back down the aisle to exit the plane. I was so confused. Then Michael handed me the hot, red box of minis across the aisle.

WHAT?! My mind was blown. I was in shock.

Tears rolled down my face as I put my head on the headrest and the plane ascended into the air with the box of minis in my hands. I thought about what had just happened and how much it meant to me. God is on the throne! He knows it all. He loves us and cares about every detail of our lives, including Chick-N-Minis®. This story still makes me weep. His goodness is so grand. He took a terrible situation and made it into something beautiful. How is Jesus reaching out to you and showing you that He is with you in every detail of your life, that He loves you and cares for you? He is waiting and wants you to see Him at work in the grand—and in the minis.

HONEY NUGGET

Even in life's heaviest moments, God delights in meeting us with small, tender reminders— proving His love is present in both the grand miracles and the tiniest details.

CHAPTER 26

COME TO ME

Here is my pain—raw and exposed. After having the most wonderful summer in San Diego, a summer that felt like a dream, it ended when I woke up to the reality that my husband and I had to go back to Dallas. A place I live but don't call home (yet). We had only been living in Dallas for seven months, so we were still figuring a lot of things out. For the month of July we went back to San Diego to see everyone while we beat the Texas heat. Our summer there was filled to the brim with beautiful gatherings, perfect weather, and being with our family and friends. My heart was overjoyed to be together, spending our days in each other's company. My heart had longed to be with family and good friends every day since we had moved away.

A few days after arriving in San Diego, we had a Fourth of July family pool celebration at our house. The boys helped me get the backyard cleaned and ready for the party. Ryan, my youngest, spent two days power washing the entire pool area. Jake, my oldest, helped me pick out plants and flowers and plant them. Luke, my middle, gave a lot of moral support and pointed out areas that needed attention. He also picked up much-needed nourishment from our favorite restaurant, Board and Brew, whose chicken sandwiches are a local Del Mar favorite, and Mexican food from our favorite local shop, Nico's. It blessed my heart that my college-age sons were so willing to help me and spend the days with me.

The day of the party was like a dream. My mom and dad arrived and I couldn't stop hugging them. I had missed them so much. Next, my brother Drew, with Renee and their three amazing kids, Carter, Katie, and Hailey, came in. These kids are the most respectful and well-behaved kids with the biggest hearts! We were all hugging and smiling, so happy to be together again. Gretchen, my sister, came in with her husband Brent and two handsome boys, Brady and Grayson. They had grown at least a foot since we saw them last and had taken every sports field on like warriors. Markus, my brother, and Ashley came in with long, heartfelt hugs and finally, Heather, my youngest sister. This is us. Nineteen of us in total, so we call ourselves K19. They are my whole heart.

My mom and dad taught me from before I can ever remember how important family is. We love and care for one another. We show up and are each other's biggest fans. I am not kidding you when I say we used to have dinner together every Sunday night for years and years. We are together as often as we can be, although it is really hard now with all the sports, conflicting schedules, and craziness of life. We try to all be together at least once a month for a meal.

So back to the pool party! It was so much fun! Besides the normal fun games in the pool and Jacuzzi, Jake somehow talked a few victims, I mean participants, into going into his converted freezer he uses daily for cold plunges. He convinced eleven of the nineteen of our family to get into the freezing cold water. It was quite the event. One after the other, they went into the plunge. The music was blaring, and the timer was reset. It was so much fun! Did I go in? No. (Side note: Remember this for the next book I write. Boy do I have a story about a cold plunge.) We all ate together, took pictures, hugged, and enjoyed the entire afternoon. I don't think I lost my smile once. I was so happy to be together again. When I went to bed that night, I fell asleep still smiling.

Our G5 family (Michael, Jake, Luke, Ryan, and I) spent much time together that summer as well. For me, it filled a space in my heart that felt vacant. I realize that children are supposed to grow up and move out and have their own families. But there is something in me that longs for G5 to be together. Yes, you can hear the boys' response now, "Mooommmmmm," every time I asked to take a G5 family picture. They really hated taking pictures, but they did it. They are my pride and joy. All I want to do is be with them and capture the moment.

Isn't that how God is with us? We are His children, and He made us as we were on His mind even before He made the universe. He designed and orchestrated everything about our life. He delights in us and just wants us to spend time with Him. He is available all the time and is just waiting for us to come to Him; that is how I feel about being with my boys, being there for them. I am human and mess up all the time, but God is God and is the perfect parent. It helps me understand Him better when I use this analogy.

The end of summer came. All the goodbyes had been said, the tears were wiped, and we were off to the airport, heading back to Dallas. I was less than a peach as I flew away from the glorious summer we had together. Instead of being grateful and thankful for the best summer ever, I was pouting. I am not proud of this, but it is part of the story. My heart hurt as I wanted to stay in San Diego with my family G5 and K19 and forever friends, but I couldn't. I held in my tears for the entire ride to the house from the airport and as I walked into the beautiful but VERY QUIET and EMPTY house. My heart was heavy. My throat hurt from holding in the emotion.

I walked straight into my closet, and the Holy Spirit said in a gentle voice to me, "Matthew 11:28." I turned my head to look around because I heard it so clearly. "Matthew 11:28." I knew that I recognized that verse. Wait, "Come to me, and I will give you rest," or something like that. I grabbed my Bible out of my bag and flipped to the Scripture.

> *Come to Me all you who labor and are*
> *heavy laden, and I will give you rest.*
> MATTHEW 11:28

The well of tears was so full it overflowed down my face. He knew. He saw me. He was encouraging me in the absolutely best way to fill my heart best.

> *Yes, Lord. You know. You know what it is like to leave Your*
> *family, to feel the pain of separation, to love someone so much*
> *and have them leave. You felt all that on the cross when it*
> *looked like God had forsaken You and left You alone to die.*
> *For three days You were alone and without Your Father, and,*
> *man, it hurt. You felt betrayed and rejected. So my heart*
> *hurts leaving my G5 and K19 and all my beautiful friends.*
> *But Jesus, You know. I am not alone.*

Do you know how much that helps me to know I am not alone in this? And you are not alone in what you are going through either. Jesus came to earth so we would know that He has gone before us and experienced it all so we would never feel lonely, abandoned, betrayed, or unloved. We have the most loving Father who, through it all, is perfect and complete. The good news is that Jesus walked this earth with us, so He knows and has felt everything we feel. He understands and has the most compassion for us. God knows it is hard and that without Him it is nearly impossible. I say all the time, "I don't know how I would get through life without the Lord."

So I gave the Lord my "burden" and focused on what He said. He said, "Come to Me." I stood in my closet and let the emotion of all my sadness come over me and showed God how much it hurt. I just wanted to be with my people. Knowing He heard me and knew my heavy heart helped me. Then I said,

> *Lord, I feel sad and so down having to leave everyone. I know You called us to Dallas, and my kids had to go back to school, and my K19 family have all their own things to do, but man—it is hard. I am going to trust You with all of them and all of this. I know You have great and mighty plans, and they are bigger and better than my ways, my plans, and my wants.*

I walked out of my closet, after having this beautiful encounter with the Lord, to feed the dog and start our life back in Dallas. I was going to be okay. He would help me. I was overwhelmed with the Holy Spirit telling me the Scripture that would help me, speaking to me in His loving, soft, gentle voice. What a good Father we have.

HONEY NUGGET

Even in the ache of goodbye, we can rest in knowing the One who loves us most understands our pain, carries our burdens, and never leaves us alone.

CHAPTER 27

SEARCHING FOR THE SAME DIAMONDS

Yes, I lost the diamond earrings AGAIN! I mean, come on! I was so careful, or so I thought. Thankfully, I am a pretty quick learner when it comes to pain, so the last time I lost my diamond earrings, after searching for hours, I remembered to ask God for help. It seems intuitive, but for me, I had to learn it the hard way. So I asked the Lord over and over to help me find these diamonds.

I first realized that they were missing when we arrived in San Diego for a long weekend, so I was pretty sure they weren't there but back in Dallas. I went ahead and searched the house. I prayed and asked the Lord, just to be safe, and they were not there. I told myself not to panic and that when we got back to Dallas, I would find them.

I casually walked into my Dallas bathroom trying to play it cool when we returned from our quick trip to San Diego to see family and friends and then started frantically looking in all the drawers. I was searching alone for these little gems because I didn't want to reveal my stupid mistake to anyone.

Lord, please, can You tell me where they are like last time?

I asked and heard crickets. I waited. I listened, but I still didn't hear anything. I could not find them. Days turned into weeks. The guilt and frustration was getting to me. I felt crazy. Were they in San Diego? I searched my photos to get some sort of eye on them, and I found them! I was wearing them on December 9. And from that point, there were no more pictures. I wore them often, so I figured I would see them if there were any pictures of me on my phone.

While Michael was at work, I did a deep dive in my closet. I spent an entire day moving and searching through EVERY item in the closet, every pocket, every bag, every drawer, every nook, everywhere. I did get some old stuff out of my closet and was able to do a deep cleaning so that was nice, but what I wanted were my diamonds that Michael had given me for my thirty-seventh birthday.

I think the part that was eating me up was that I was at the point where I knew I had to tell my husband. These diamond earrings were a precious gift from him, and I did not want him to be disappointed in me or think that I didn't take good care of them. For weeks, I bit my tongue and didn't tell Michael. I continued to search, hoping I could keep it a secret and no one would ever find out.

Unfortunately, I accidentally told my sister Heather on the phone one afternoon—something I immediately regretted. I could find them on my own. I had to find them. I thought I needed to keep it a secret to protect myself, that I could take care of it in my own strength. Yes,

I asked the Lord for help, but I still hadn't found them. I was for sure not going to tell anyone else about my mistake. Pretty sure this goes with my perfectionism, but it was eating me alive. But isn't that what sin is—it is this nasty, little thing that we want to hide from everyone else. We want to keep it a secret, and then it spirals into more lies. I was at the point of sheer mental and physical exhaustion, trying to remember where I put the earrings and unearthing my whole bedroom, bathroom, and closet in Dallas.

They had been missing for two months, and I convinced myself they were in San Diego and not in Dallas. So we went back to San Diego for a visit to see our family and our good friends. While we were there, I hunted for the diamonds in the house. I excavated my bathroom, deep into all the crannies and crevices—but they were nowhere to be found. Mind you, I still have only told my sister on accident, and no one else. I was still all alone in this secret.

A few days later we were back in Dallas, and all the boys were there to watch Luke's SMU lacrosse game and celebrate Ryan's twenty-first birthday. These young men know me so well and are the biggest encouragement to me. I just adore my boys and relish any time I have with them. It is so reminiscent of our long days together in London when we worked so hard at school and spent hours together every day. I think it was my comfort and ease with them that led me to blurt out that I had lost my earrings. It was like I couldn't hold it in one more moment. A volcano erupted. The information was like hot lava that was boiling inside me, eating me alive from the inside out. They were concerned and asked the big question, "Did you tell Dad?" Ahhhh, no, I hadn't, but I needed to. I had to tell him to get the burden off of me! They urged me to tell him right away.

Two are better than one,
Because they have a good reward for their labor.
For if they fall, one will lift up his companion.
But woe to him who is alone when he falls,
For he has no one to help him up.

ECCLESIASTES 4:9-10

Here is the God moment; are you ready? The boys had all gone back to school and their homes, and Michael had gotten home from work. I was going to finally tell him the truth. We were both getting ready in the bathroom before we went out to dinner when I decided to reveal my mistake. I explained how I had been searching and couldn't find the earrings anywhere, and I had been searching in both houses for three months. I said, "I always put them in the exact same spot when I take them off and put them right here in my top drawer in the container next to my toothbrush and toothpaste" as I pulled open the drawer to show him. Guess what? THEY WERE RIGHT THERE NESTLED AGAINST ALL THE OTHER JEWELRY! They were exactly where I always put them three months prior! I had looked a zillion times over! And yes, I do brush my teeth twice a day, and somehow I could not see them for the hundred times I had looked and pulled open that drawer.

What I learned from this experience was to get the junk, the hurt, the sin, the problem you are dealing with out of you by telling God and trusted people. I told God first, but I believe He challenged me by taking me to the point of being sick with regret and disappointment before I was able to tell my trusted people. We can't do this alone. God is my good Father, He loves me so much, and He gave me some very special people to love me regardless of the dumb things I do and the mistakes I make. I had been so afraid to admit to Michael I lost the diamonds and had made a mistake. For what? I was in anguish internally for months looking for those diamonds. I am not saying I would have found them earlier, but the release I felt from telling and talking to my trusted people helped me so much.

Why was I tackling this alone? God did not put us here on earth to stuff all of our burdens, insecurities, pain, and embarrassment inside of us. He gave us each other to help us through, even when we do silly things, because He knows we need people just as much as we need Him. What do you need to share with a trusted person in your life?

HONEY NUGGET

True freedom is found when we stop hiding our burdens and let God and the people He's given us, carry them with us.

CHAPTER 28

MY FOURTH SON

I always wanted to have four kids. However, due to difficulties in my pregnancies, the doctors advised against having any more kids. I would be on bed rest the entire pregnancy—and that still wouldn't guarantee a healthy birth. We felt it was not fair to my other three boys if I was in bed for nine months because little boys need their mom! So the dream of four kids was squashed. I was so grateful for my three handsome sons, who were healthy and strong. Instead of dwelling on a dream I had that had been changed and getting bitter about it, I chose to instead be grateful for what I did have—three beautiful gifts from the Lord!

> *I will praise You, for [they are] fearfully and*
> *wonderfully made; marvelous are Your works!*
> PSALM 139:14

After that advice, we never thought about having another child because we trusted the doctors and had been through so much with

Ryan. But no one said we couldn't adopt! To add to our little family of five, we adopted a little bundle of pure joy named Xander. He is a little, white Maltese Poodle. Xander was just a two-and-a-half-pound fluffball when we rescued him from a pet store, but over time, he grew to eighteen pounds. The weekend we got him was just after moving back to San Diego after living in London for three years. The boys were all in elementary school and the perfect age to help take care of him. To clarify, we were not planning to get a dog. He was a total surprise to us! We went up to Newport Beach for a fun weekend away to celebrate Father's Day; it is one of our favorite places and things to do as a family.

We casually popped into a pet store while waiting for dinner one night at Fashion Island Shopping Center. I was cuddling him when I asked the employee if it was a girl or a boy. Picture the biggest smile on my face when he said it was a boy. Of course, another boy. I was in love! Michael was warming up to the thought, and the boys loved him. Who wouldn't? I did, and I can honestly say I was not a dog person at all. During our long weekend away, we would go for long bike rides along the ocean and bay of Balboa Island and Newport Beach. Michael would lead the pack, and the boys would follow while I was at the back. We would stop for lunch and ice cream and enjoy every moment. Michael and I prayed and asked and waited and wondered about getting the dog. We didn't want to get the boys excited about getting him until we were decided.

Lord, help! Is this a good decision for our family? Is this wise? Is this what You want us to do?

Not sure if we heard from the Lord on this one or not, to be super honest here. We didn't hear any Scripture, but we sure didn't get any red flags NOT to get him either. I mean, come on: He was a white, fluffy ball of warmth and goodness that felt so snuggly to hold and so fun to watch and love. Every day, we went to visit him at the mall's pet store. Every time we went to see him, our hearts fell deeper in love. By the last day of our trip, we had a fourth son! What an adventure!

Back at home, he quickly felt right at home. He was a lot of work, but it was such a perfect time to get an energizer bunny, I mean puppy! He was so tiny; he would run around our couch and fit underneath it without even ducking his head. He chewed everything we left out, including Michael's favorite pair of sunglasses (oops!) and the frame of the back door. Xander was an expensive little guy but worth every penny. We had the time to care for him and the house to keep him. We also knew this was a long commitment, but we were ready for it. He took over my heart immediately. Maybe I was a dog person, and I didn't know it yet.

I did not realize the companionship he would bring me personally. Truth be told, I knew he would be a responsibility and would stay at home with me, but I never expected him to follow me everywhere I went. Is this normal to have an animal understand you, love you, and want to be with you? Our summer was the best one yet with this little guy. In the fall, all the boys were back in traditional school for the first time, and I was at home with no homeschoolers to school. So this little guy had my full attention, and I was quickly so grateful to have him home with me. I didn't feel alone like I thought I might after the boys went to school.

Because of this, I believe the Lord blessed me with Xander in so many ways. He knew before I even knew what I needed. This dog is always by my side. We talk and chit-chat all day long about different things, like *who is at the door?* and *when is Dad coming home?* He reminds me so much of Diana, my mother-in-law, in the very best ways. They love to just "be" with me. I would literally stand up, and she would stand up. I would look outside, and she would look outside. When I was newly married, to be honest, it would drive me a little crazy, but I tried to embrace it as the years went by. She definitely kept me on my toes when she came to visit. But she was just concerned and interested in what I was doing and why, wanting to be a part of my life. Just like Xander.

Isn't that just like the Lord? He is available and wants to be in every part of our life when we stop and invite Him in and "let Him." Regardless of what is happening in our life, God is with us if we have put our trust in Him!

> *For the Lord your God is with you wherever you go.*
> JOSHUA 1:9

I can say I have learned so much about love from my dog. The way he loves me reminds me that God loves me in some of the same ways. Unconditionally. Always eager, always pursuing, always loving without an "If you do this, I will do that." He is never out to get me or make me sad or suffer; all He does is love me for who I am. He delights in me. Unconditional love is unlike conditional love. Conditional love says if you do this, then I will do that. It puts limits and conditions on love and makes you feel unworthy as if you need to earn it. If I could only impress, perform, and do to perfection, then I would gain your love. So many relationships are broken and segmented from this kind of conditional love. It is like running on a hamster wheel—it is exhausting and hard. This is what we do as humans.

Thankfully, the Lord's character is not like this at all. We don't have to do anything to earn His love as it is a free gift because of who He is, not because of who we are or what we do. Take a deep breath and let that truth sink in. God loves us unconditionally because of who He is, not because of what we have done. That truth changes everything.

Let's fast forward thirteen years to the present, and Xander is moving a little slower. He has some arthritis and stiffness in his joints. One night he was lying with me on the couch when I said I was going to get him some treats for his playmat, where I hid treats, and he had to find them. He jumped off the couch to follow me to the kitchen and stopped in his tracks. He screamed so loud and for so long, and we could see he couldn't put his weight on his back leg. We scooped him up and headed for the ER. They did a fantastic job of helping mitigate the pain and figure out what was wrong with his leg. That night, we left with pain meds and felt satisfied that he would be okay. Well, friends, he was not okay.

Over the next few days, he did not eat, was up every hour to go outside to go potty, and was super lethargic. I took him to the vet three consecutive days, saying he was not okay. Something else is wrong with him besides his "broken" leg. I knew him, and he was not right. But on the fifth day of no improvement whatsoever, the vet wanted to keep him for the day, monitor him, and do a scan to see if they could find anything out. This is where I say life is hard, and it just got harder. I have heard so many times when you get a diagnosis from a doctor, the whole room starts spinning and your focus gets super myopic. That afternoon when I went back to pick up Xander, it happened to me. They called me back into the room to wait for the doctor, where they brought Xander, and he was happy and sniffing the room. He was so happy to see me. I offered him a treat

(I packed a day bag for him to have for the day he spent there). He ate it. I was so relieved because I had not seen him eat in five days. I quickly texted Jake and said, "He is eating treats! God answered your prayers!" But I tried not to get ahead of myself.

At the same time, Michael was on his way to the vet to meet me to pick him up because I had this feeling I didn't want to be there alone. This was not like me at all. I am usually totally capable of handling this on my own, but there was something deep inside me that knew there was a problem. I am going to go ahead and give the Holy Spirit the credit here for leading me to ask Michael to come meet me at the vet after work. Before Michael arrived, the vet who had seen me the last three days said, "I have some really bad news." Literally, the tears turned on like a fire hose. "No," I kept saying, "no, no, no. My husband is on his way too, and I want to wait for him." But then I couldn't wait. Bad news. How did a somewhat simple leg injury turn into a statement from the vet that said, "I have some really bad news to report?"

Lord, no. What is happening? Help, Lord! Help!

I insisted on hearing the news before Michael could arrive. My life changed forever in that moment. The vet said, "We found tumors on the ultrasound. They are in his stomach, esophagus, pancreas, and lymph nodes. They are quite large and have probably been there a while." The pain meds irritated the tumors and caused the bleeding and the other issues he had been experiencing. It was devastating news to receive. Yes, I understand he was a dog, but he was more than a dog. Xander was my gift from the Lord, and he was my fourth son.

The night we received the life-altering news, I could not sleep—not even a wink until 4:30 a.m., when I think I dozed off for an hour. I was consumed with worry, fear, and sadness. It was the worst; the pain I felt for him was overwhelming. I wished that it could have been me instead of him. He was a dog. He didn't deserve this, and he couldn't tell me if he was in pain or not. My motherly instinct felt so weak, and I felt like a failure. I had no idea he was fighting this battle on his own, and if the tumors were that large, it had been a while, the vet guessed. I was so sad for him, so concerned that he was miserable and had no way of telling me.

> *Lord, please help Xander and comfort him. Lord, help him with the pain, and please help me to know when he is in pain so I can help.*

Twenty-four hours after receiving the heartbreaking news, we were home with him, celebrating when he ate his food. Michael and I cracked a smile and high-fived when he went #2 outside normally. We were celebrating the small things. Praise Jesus! It felt good to smile and make a joke after all the seriousness of the past day. At bedtime I left Xander and Michael on the couch in the family room to get ready for bed. At that point we had to carry him everywhere because his back knee was still dislocated, and he was in pain from walking. So Michael kept the dog on the couch so he wouldn't follow me into my room. He had said a few times, "Let's remember all the good times and focus on the positive things now." I was trying, but all I could think about was if he was suffering and in pain. I couldn't imagine life without my constant companion by my side. I was so upset and cried gallons of tears for him. I am sure Michael was overwhelmed with me as well because I couldn't shake it.

Which reminds me, did you know that the Lord collects every single tear that falls from our eyes? I mean, seriously? He sees and cares deeply for each of us. He is going to have to get a super-sized vat for my tears because when I am alone with Him, I let Him see how I am feeling, and my tears overflow in His presence.

You number my wanderings; put my tears into Your bottle.
PSALM 56:8

While I went to put on my pajamas and brush my teeth, I was talking with the Lord, and I felt like the Holy Spirit spoke to me in His sweet voice, reminding me of a familiar Scripture:

Finally, brethren, whatever things are true, whatever things are noble, whatever things are just, whatever things are pure, whatever things are lovely, whatever things are of good report, if there is any virtue and if there is anything praiseworthy—meditate on these things.
PHILIPPIANS 4:8

Yes, Lord, that's exactly what I should do with this absolutely heartbreaking news.

I knew the gist of the Scripture but had to get my Bible to read it word for word. It was the same Scripture the Lord had shown me before, so I knew it well, but in a different context (see chapter 20, "Freedom from Lies: All Men Cheat").

I needed to cherish all the memories of Xander, hug my little guy a little tighter, and stop worrying and fabricating in my mind what *could* happen. It was driving me wild. I had to stop. I was afraid that my sweet Xander would pass away before his brothers could see him again or that he would never get to visit San Diego with us again. From that moment until now, as I write this with him lying at my feet, I have felt a peace that I cannot explain. My dog is dying; I don't know when, but I have peace. And in true Jesus miracle-making-fashion, all his brothers have seen him numerous times, AND every time we go back to San Diego, he has gone too. He has now lived another 19 months and counting.

The first time back in San Diego with him as we drove by the beautiful downtown San Diego harbor with the skyline in the background and the warm breeze blowing through the open window, he sat in my lap in the Uber. I held Xander, thanking God that I was able to take him "home" again. Tears of joy. Tears of gratitude. Jesus heard my heart and saw my requests. Some might say it is silly, but for me, my Father heard my heart.

HONEY NUGGET

God often answers our deepest prayers not with words but with the tender unfolding of moments that show He has heard the cries of our heart.

CHAPTER 29

PRAYING FOR PARKING SPOTS

Sounds super shallow and selfish to pray for parking spots, I know. It is a need we have to get where we are going, and it seems so frivolous when there are hurting people with far more issues than a parking spot. At one time I felt like it wasn't worth it to even ask. Who am I? And a parking spot? Silly! *I will save my prayer for something bigger and better that is more important. I will save my prayer for something big or for someone else.*

Maybe you think this way about asking God for a need you have. We think our requests are too small and unimportant or we aren't important enough. But if we change our perspective to who is answering this prayer, it will diminish those myths and lies. Who is God, and what is His character? God is all-loving, powerful, and good. He is the best Father and gives us perfect gifts from above as James 1:17 says. Everything good in our lives is from the Lord!

Speaking of good gifts from God, do I have a story for you. At the time of this story, my mom was pregnant with my youngest sibling. My dad knew I would love to be in the delivery room because I was sixteen years old and the oldest in our family. My dad always did a great job exposing us to places and events that would help to shape us. So I am sure he thought, *Lets throw her in a delivery room and have her see how babies are born.* He said I could come back to the hospital after I took my siblings back home. I had brought all the kids to see Mom for a quick visit in the hospital. At the time, I had two brothers and one sister: Drew was fourteen years old, Gretchen was seven, and Markus was three.

I was driving my mom's huge blue van to and from the hospital with all the kids, the built-in nanny with the mom van. No offense if you drive a minivan, but I never had one because of this blue van. It was enormous and so not cool for a sixteen-year-old girl to drive. And to top it all off, it had two pheasants on the two back windows. Urg! It did get me from point A to point B, and that was all my dad said was important. Well, that resulted in no minivans for me when I had my own kids. Haha!

So it was just me and the pheasants in the blue van racing back to the hospital to my mom's labor and delivery room to witness the most miraculous event of life: childbirth! It was also the biggest surprise of all surprises. The doctors all believed my mom was having a baby boy because of the baby's low heart rate. They had already had his name picked out—Michael Andrew. You guessed it, when that baby came out, that baby was not a boy but a girl! We could not believe it. My parents were shocked and didn't even have a name for her. I was elated! A second baby sister to play with and dress up and love on. I quickly started brainstorming names for her to suggest to my parents. I came up with Heather Suzanne for her name. Heather, because of my dad, Henry, and myself, Heidi. And for her middle name, Suzanne, a derivative of Susan. They bought it, and that is how I named my sister!

Since that June day in 1987, I have been enamored with her. She is a gift, like all my siblings. I cherish each of them—Drew, Gretchen, Markus, and now Heather! I say all of this because it is why we spend so much time together. We do life together, and it is so fun! Our group text name is FAB5 because I think they are the most fabulous siblings in the world. I love them.

One day, not too long ago, Heather and I were heading from her place to the mall to go shopping. We both had to take our cars, so of course the moment we started driving, we were on the phone together because you know we always had things to talk about. As we approached the mall this particularly sunny and very busy afternoon, we discovered all of San Diego was also at the mall trying to shop. We drove into the lower, dark level of the parking garage. This was going to be tough to not only find one spot but two! I said my prayer to the Lord so casually but expectantly, because He hears all of our prayers, out loud while we were still on the phone after our thirty-minute commute.

I said something like,

> *Lord, would You please help us find a place to park? Today, we need two spots. If You don't mind, can You help us park close together? Amen.*

Heather was in front of me, had driven down the aisle, and had disappeared. Within a moment, I saw a lady climb into her car, and I turned on my blinker. I had one! I screamed with excitement to have secured a spot. We were still on the phone when I saw two guys come out and climb into their car in front of my parked car. "Heather, I don't know where you are now, but there are two guys leaving in the next aisle. Hurry, drive down the aisle and look to the right." I was so frantic I wasn't sure what I was saying or seeing. It was like slow motion. Heather yelled, "I got a spot!"

She didn't know where I had pulled in, but I saw. A smile on my face grew full when I realized what had just happened. I watched her pull in. Our cars would be nose to nose. Are you kidding me, Lord?

"Heather, look up!" I said while I was climbing out of my car. She saw my car in front of hers. It was so God. We kept saying we couldn't believe that happened the whole walk into the mall.

So why can't we pray for a parking spot? We can. He is faithful and hears our every cry. God doesn't have any limits. He doesn't have a quota to reach or only a handful of yes votes for prayers. God is good. That means He will do only what is good. He can do no evil. Everything good, wonderful, beautiful, pure, and noble in your life and mine is because of God.

Every time I pray for a parking spot and one opens up, I am overwhelmed again by His goodness. There is also a shift in my thinking, whether the ideal, close spot opens up or I have to wait a bit and park a bit farther away. It is okay. Maybe the driver behind me is pregnant or bringing their elderly dad, and they need a closer spot. Perhaps He wants me in my car longer so I can learn to be more patient and trust His timing. He knows what is best, and I have surrendered it to Him. Regardless, He is good, loving, and knows what is best. So this parking spot is an example of everything we need to pray for in our lives.

Be anxious for nothing, but in everything by
prayer and supplication, with thanksgiving, let
your requests be made known to God.

PHILIPPIANS 4:6

They are just easy, very quick needs that we can see God answer. But what about the harder things in life? We can trust Him with it all, the easy and the hard. For me, parking spots are faith-builders and opportunities to remind myself that God can do all things!

HONEY NUGGET

Even the smallest prayers matter to God because
His love for you is as big as His power—nothing
in your life is too small for His attention.

CHAPTER 30

WAY MAKER

The four men in my life—Michael, Jake, Luke, and Ryan—have each taught me profound lessons about life, myself, and the Lord. Through them, I've learned to trust God in deeper ways and to see His hand at work in every season. There's a beautiful song, "Way Maker" by Leeland, that captures the journey we've walked together. Each of their stories reflects one of God's remarkable qualities revealed in that song—His strength, faithfulness, and unchanging nature. Time and again, I've witnessed God perform marvelous and miraculous works in their lives. Whenever I play that song on repeat, it reminds me of His goodness and the incredible things He has done.

Jake's story is a powerful reminder that God truly is a "way maker"—opening paths we could never imagine. During his sophomore year at Chapman University, Jake faced a tough season of his life. In the midst of a difficult breakup, he fought to stay focused and finish his classes strong. Just when the road ahead seemed impossible, the unexpected happened; the world shut down because of COVID-19, sending every student home. What could have been a setback became a turning point. Jake finished his spring semester from home, then after seeking God's guidance he made the bold decision not to return that fall. Instead, he took a gap year to reset, working at MD7, pursuing the Lord wholeheartedly, and rebuilding his life from the inside out. In that season, Jake emerged stronger, healthier, and deeply grounded in his identity in Jesus Christ. He transferred to University of San Diego for his junior year where he thrived academically, personally, and spiritually. He not only excelled in his studies but also set new life goals, walking in the unshakable truth of who he is in Christ. God had made a way that was far better than anything we could have planned, and Jake seized it with strength, courage, and faith.

Ryan's story had to be of a "miracle worker." As I shared in chapter 12, he entered this world without life, yet today, he stands tall, strong, and courageous. My once fragile, premature baby has grown into a determined, resilient young man who has stared down more health battles than most will face in a lifetime. If you know Ryan now, you know he is tough as nails. The rubber bracelet on his wrist reads "Never Quit," and he lives those words every day. He's run multiple marathons and, just this year, crossed the finish line of his first half-Ironman. Ryan just graduated from Baylor University this past spring. Preemies like Ryan fight uphill from their first breath, overcoming obstacles just to stand where others begin. His life is a living, breathing testament to the power, faithfulness, and goodness of God.

Luke's story beautifully demonstrates God as the ultimate "promise keeper." When Luke graduated from high school at eighteen, the Lord gave me a specific promise. I wrote the Scripture on a notecard and taped it inside my bathroom cabinet so I could see it every day to be a constant reminder that God always fulfills His Word.

Let us hold fast the confession of our hope without
wavering for He who promised is faithful.
HEBREWS 10:23

From a mother's heart, here's what I was holding onto: God promised to protect Luke from evil and danger whether he was at school here or studying abroad. He promised to be with Luke and to keep him close to His heart. And God did exactly that. Four years later, when Luke graduated from SMU, he chose to attend a five-month Youth with a Mission program in Kona, Hawaii, the very same campus and Crossroads Discipleship Training School that Michael and I had attended twenty-two years before. Talk about a full-circle moment! Now he is working in San Diego using his finance degree and surfing every day with his friends. God continues to amaze me with the good plans and faithful promises He has for each of us, which is what I am witnessing in Luke's life.

Last but not least, Michael is my example of God being "light in the darkness." God brought Michael into my life, three times over, before I could see the light. I was living in darkness, but he pointed me to the light. This man is the reason I know and love Jesus. He was so gentle and loving in the way he exemplified how a Christian would seek God. My life with Michael has far exceeded the life I ever expected to have. He makes my heart flutter, and my life is better in every way. I am forever grateful for my ruggedly handsome husband who leads our family with strength and love.

These four titles are some of the characteristics of God. He has so many beautiful names and characteristics that help us understand who He is. What stories in your life show God's character brightly? What has happened in your life that you have seen God as a way maker, a miracle worker, a promise keeper, and a light in the darkness? Looking for Him, seeing Him, seeking Him is so incredible. He is all around us; in our circumstances we just need to look for Him. Someday, when we get to heaven after putting our trust in Him, we will see the full picture of our abundant lives with all the ways the Lord has woven goodness into our broken lives. I just think why not ask Him now because He is waiting to reveal Himself to us. Seeking God will change everything about your perspective of your story like it did mine.

HONEY NUGGET

God's fingerprints are all over our stories, weaving His way-making, miracle-working, promise-keeping, light-giving love into every chapter of our lives.

CHAPTER 31

SWEET BLESSINGS

I would be remiss not to update y'all on our move to Dallas now that we have been in Texas for three and a half years. I spoke earlier of the blessing of our big move of being reunited with our best friends and family in San Diego when we would come back for a visit, but there is so much more that I can see now because I have been hunting for honey.

One of the first things we did in 2021 when we arrived was to find a great church. There are so many great churches in Texas that we thought the search might take months. When we moved to London with the Christenson's, we visited eight churches before we found the one we all liked, remember there were nine of us. Instead, finding a church here was love at first visit with Watermark Community Church. It is a huge church, but we felt like we were home from our first Sunday morning. I turned to Michael during the worship and said to him, "This is why we moved here!" My heart was overwhelmed with the intimate worship that my soul longed for.

We had found Watermark, no kidding, from a Dallas influencer I followed on Instagram after she posted TA's (Pastor Timothy Ateek) handle and a photo of him preaching. He said he had just moved to Dallas with his wife and three boys, which resonated with me. I clicked on the link, which took me to that Sunday's message. I watched it and loved it, then sent it to Michael. He agreed it was excellent. Later that week Luke came by the house for a visit and told us about a great church he went to called... Watermark. He had gone to The Porch (the college-age ministry group) on Tuesday night with some SMU friends. Funny how that all happened. Looked like God's fingerprints all over it to me.

Shortly after that first Sunday, I joined the women's Bible study that met every Wednesday morning. It was February 2022 when I bravely walked in and sat with my group that had been together since the previous September. It was hard for me to join midyear and walk in alone, but I did it. My mindset was focused on God. He went with me, so I was never alone. I knew I would find some sisters in Christ here so the initial feeling of being uncomfortable would all be worth it.

From this women's Bible study over the next two years, friendships bloomed and blossomed, and five of us women and our husbands formed a community group. We meet as a group every other week for dinner and fellowship. The deep friendship and intimacy that we have with this group is more than I ever thought or imagined it could be. We literally do life together, celebrate the highs of life and help each other with the lows. We do it all together as we walk through life with our marriages, kids, jobs, etc. The women also meet up for lunch, breakfast, nails, coffee, prayer, you name it. We have the best time together! The men have also formed a strong bond, built on trust, faith, and friendship. This small group is an answer to prayer to have close friends to point us to Jesus and remind us who we are in Him. Jennie Allen said, "You and I need friends who, instead of trying to fix us, help us to fix our eyes more firmly on Jesus."[13] This is exactly what this group of friends is like.

My soul longed for these friendships. I didn't know that I had this hole in my heart that was shaped like a small community group of friendship and fellowship, but the Lord did. I had this longing and desire to be in a relationship with others that knew me, cared for me, and accepted me. Our Creator, who made us, knew we had this desire and knew how to fill it. I am guessing you have this same hole. Do you have a few close friends to talk about Jesus and walk through life with one another? It will bless you in ways you never thought it would. Pastor Rick Warren of Saddleback Church always sounded like a broken record about being in a small group. I get it now. This group fills a gap in my heart that is so beautiful and so life-giving. Pastor Rick was right. And this is what the Lord says about friendship:

> *Iron sharpens iron, and one man*
> *[or woman] sharpens another.*
> **Proverbs** 27:17 esv

Another source of sweetness in my life has come from a wonderful group of women I met in Dallas. It all started when I met a neighbor from the next street over whose husband developed the building where Michael leased office space for MD7. She and I connected instantly, and a genuine friendship began to form. We discovered how much we enjoyed doing life together. We both liked working out (though I nearly fainted during our very first class, which was admittedly mortifying!), shopping, lingering over lunches, and simply savoring each other's company. Funny enough, her neighbor across the street and my neighbor across the street knew each other. We all started playing mahjong, the best game ever invented, but more importantly, it opened the door to sweet friendships and fun weekly girl time together. Now we not only play mahjong but also enjoy lunches together, go on walks, bake sourdough bread, and take part in fun events around Dallas.

These two groups of friends have been so soul quenching to me. The Lord knew me and the desire I had to find friends. The hole in my heart was a crater sized hole when we moved away from all of my friends in San Diego. I really thought I would never have good friends like them in Dallas. Oh, the Lord was probably just smiling down at me because He was working behind the scenes.

> *Delight yourself in the Lord, and he will*
> *give you the desires of your heart.*
> PSALM 37:4 ESV

My San Diego friends are irreplaceable and such a huge gift to me that I cherish and adore with all of my heart. I have been blessed with these friends who have walked beside me for years. These friends know me deeply and love me anyway. Their encouragement sharpens me and makes me a better person. They have shaped me into a better wife, mom, daughter, and friend, simply by being who they are and reminding me of whom I want to be. I can only thank God for weaving such steadfast, soul-filling friendships into my story. They are my joy. They are a gift. Friendships are the sweetness of life like a drizzle of honey on peanut butter toast.

I thank my God upon every remembrance of you.

PHILIPPIANS 1:3

On top of our church, our community group, and amazing new friends, I have another huge blessing in my life that resulted from moving to Dallas. It is between Michael and me. I know you have read about a lot of our life together and the heartaches and celebrations we have had along the way, and I would not pick anyone else to do life with. We have, I would say, a very awesome marriage that we are both grateful for and thrilled with. We have gone through a lot together, with the boys, with the businesses, with the moves, with our families, with life. We try our very best to stay close to the Lord and always try to seek Him throughout it all.

Abide in Me and I in you. As the branch cannot
bear fruit of itself, unless it abides in the vine,
neither can you, unless you abide in Me.

JOHN 15:4

When we moved to Dallas, we came as empty nesters. All our chicks were in college, and we were alone. Do you know what happened to our marriage? It got even sweeter than before. Every day felt like a celebration with him. I couldn't wait to see him walk in the door at night, and when he left in the morning, we were already missing each other. The Lord has knit our hearts together so tightly during this season like they have never been before. God was preparing this time for us together to bring us so much joy. Remember how crabby I was about moving? I didn't know all of the sweet blessings of moving here. I was busy worrying about my comfort and not trusting my life to the Lord. Yet again, He proved He was trustworthy.

As the Father loved Me, I also have loved you; abide in My love. If you keep My commandments, you abide in My love, just as I have kept My Father's commandments and abide in His love. These things I have spoken to you, that My joy may remain in you, and that your joy may be full.

JOHN 15:9-11

HONEY NUGGET

The One who created our hearts knows exactly how to fill them with what we truly need.

CHAPTER 32

THE HOUSE
IS ON FIRE

The most recent God story to share is that our forever home in San Diego caught on fire. Yes, you are reading that correctly. Our home of twenty-five years went up in smoke and flames. Our neighbor saw the smoke coming from the rooftop of our home one Saturday afternoon. He ran down the hill to our front door and was alternating between incessantly ringing the doorbell and banging on the front door, all while he simultaneously called 911 on speaker phone. I saw the whole thing unfold on our Ring doorbell from Dallas. It was incredible and literally made me hold my breath in disbelief!

It was a silent fire that started in the fireplace walls and chimney and snuck into the wall spaces of the house, the attic, and roof. No alarms went off because the fire and smoke were enclosed in the walls.

Jake and Luke were the only ones living there at the time. When Michael and I moved to Dallas, Jake was living there alone to finish up college. He was the property manager per se and was able to get to University of San Diego in only twenty minutes. What a gift for all of us. Now both Jake and Luke have graduated from college and work in San Diego, so they live in the house together.

Luke and one of his friends were watching a movie in the family room. It was so unlike them to be watching TV on a beautiful Saturday afternoon, but Luke had injured his back and had only been home from the hospital for a few days before the fire. He was moving slowly, so his friend offered to come over so he wouldn't be alone. Oh, thank You, Lord, for this protection! Jake made a fire in the fireplace for them since it was chilly in the house and left to see some other friends for the afternoon. The fire must have started shortly after this.

The fire was big enough to make the local news, and five fire trucks and their crews showed up in response. We live next to open space filled with brush and trees, so I am sure they were being extra cautious so this house fire didn't morph into a wildfire situation that is so prevalent in Southern California. The fire destroyed about two-thirds of our house, either by fire, smoke, or water damage.

After three hours of sheer craziness, the fire trucks left. Because the damage was extensive enough, the power and water were shut off, and our house was deemed unlivable. Luke and Jake had the clothes on their backs and grabbed a few smoky items from their rooms and left. The family room and living room walls were completely torched. Upstairs the destruction was worse. It demolished our master bathroom, closet, room, laundry room, boys' bathroom, Ryan's room, and the entire attic and roof. All were burnt, charred, smoked, and drenched with water.

The boys had to go stay at a friend's house, and our forever home was left empty. As I write this story, they are currently in a nearby rental, and we are waiting for permits and the insurance to even start rebuilding. It is going to be at least another year before we can move back in. It was a lot to deal with not only physically but emotionally as well. Our forever home, as I keep calling it, is where we have raised our boys, celebrated every holiday, and gone through every up and down of life. Oh boy, did we need the Lord to get through this fire, this storm, this unexpected tragedy.

There is more to this story…as you are used to my stories by now in this book. You see, on this very precious afternoon, it was also the birthday of my miracle baby. It was March 8, 2025. Ryan turned twenty-two that day, and now it is also marked the day of the fire. This day is already a hard day for me as I remember how my body gave into labor and my sweet two-pound boy was born. But I cannot forget how faithful God was on this day either. It is bittersweet.

And there is even more to the story…another tragedy happened on this day when Ryan turned eighteen years old, March 8, 2021. This is the first time I have spoken of it in this book, although it is a huge part of our family's story and heart. We lost Michael's younger brother Chris unexpectedly on March 8. It was devastating, horrible, and shocking. It pierced our hearts like no one or anything had before. There is not a day that we don't think of Chris as he was a huge part of all of our lives.

The boys all loved Uncle Chris for so many reasons. He taught each boy how to work out in the gym. I mean WORK OUT! He was a specimen himself and knew how to transform bodies into machines. So tough and strong on the outside, and if you knew him, you knew how big his heart was on the inside. He loved everyone fiercely and made you feel seen and understood. His hugs engulfed you with love. I can feel his embrace right now. Because God is good and He is so brilliant and can make good out of any bad situation, we chose to celebrate that day knowing it is the day Michael's brother met Jesus face to face and went to heaven. His heart was made whole again, both physically and emotionally. That is the best news ever and helps our own hearts heal and find peace on earth while we were left behind.

So this precious day is even more taxing for us now with the added event of the fire. I told the Lord I was holding onto His promise so tightly and expecting Him to speak and show up. No matter what happens, the Lord is our foundation that we can trust not to change or crumble. No matter what storms come our way, even when they all come on that same day, pile up, and cause so much destruction, we can still stand on His truth, His foundation, and will not falter.

> *And the rain descended, the floods came, and*
> *the winds blew and beat on that house; and it*
> *did not fall, for it was founded on the rock.*
> MATTHEW 7:25

I was a busy little bee hunting for honey. Seeking and finding the good in the bad. The sweet in the bittersweet. The growth in the tragedy. The beauty for ashes. The ashes have a whole new meaning to me now, as you can imagine.

> *To console those who mourn in Zion, to give them*
> ***beauty for ashes,** the oil of joy for mourning, the*
> *garment of praise for the spirit of heaviness; that*
> *they may be called trees of righteousness, the*
> *planting of the Lord, that He may be glorified.*
> ISAIAH 61:3 EMPHASIS ADDED

From the afternoon that Luke called me to say, "The house is on fire," I had a recurring thought and a truth that kept coming to my mind: "God allowed this fire to happen." He didn't cause it or do it to us. Yes, He could have stopped it, but He didn't. He is using this fire to reach us and shape us and work it into something good. If God is a good Father, He is working all things out for our good. He is so loving and so clever, allowing this hardship to happen and strengthen our character. He is gently shaping what we will have for eternity: our soul and our character. We live in a broken world, and our twenty-five-year-old chimney had taken enough heat over the years and simply cracked, allowing the fire to escape into the walls of the house. It was a simple accident.

My brethren, count it all joy when you fall into various
trials, knowing the testing of your faith produces
patience. But let patience have its perfect work, that
you may be perfect and complete, lacking nothing.
JAMES 1:2-4

The morning BEFORE the fire, during my Bible reading and prayer time, I found a Scripture that I had previously read and had a sad face next to it because it reminded me of having to move to Texas. Because I now have a different perspective on our move and the blessing of being in Texas, I read that same Scripture again and fell in love with it. The Scripture just jumped off the page and hit my heart so differently. I wrote it out in my journal and took a picture of it to make the verse my new screensaver on my phone.

I would have lost heart, unless I had believed that I would
see the goodness of the Lord in the land of the living.
PSALM 27:13-14

Look at that beautiful claim that grounded my heart. The Lord knew I would need it only six hours later when I got the phone call. I had never made Scripture my phone's wallpaper until that morning. The Holy Spirit was speaking to my heart and preparing me, grounding me in the truth and the rock on which I stood.

It has been five months since the fire, and already there is so much good we see. We are so grateful; it could have been so much worse. We continuously repeat, "Thank God it didn't happen at night. It would have been a different outcome." Who knows when the fire alarms in the house would have gone off. It was silent as it roared through the enclosed framework of the house and in the attic space. The two boys' rooms are in the front of the house and face the street. The fire happened on the back side of the house, which is also where the staircase is located. My mind can very easily head south and worry about what could have happened if they were sound asleep. I am choosing to be so thankful the fire happened in the middle of the afternoon and on the weekend when neighbors were around to help.

I will be very real with you. I still felt uneasy, unstable, incredibly sad, and wobbly about the fire. I cried for my forever home. I know I didn't live there anymore, but my boys did, and I loved my house. It was just really hard to see pictures of the destruction of my beautiful home. I wanted my house back to how it was. I was holding onto it very tightly. Michael wasn't affected the same way I was. He was so strong. He is just built differently. He wasted no time and dove into the massive task of getting our house back to new.

We flew into town to see our house and meet with an insurance adjuster for a few days just a week after the fire. Jake and Luke were so strong and absolutely solid in their faith. In a moment of weakness in my destroyed bathroom, where Jake could see the tears welling in my eyes as I remembered so many memories of the past twenty-five years, Jake pulled me aside and said, "Mom, do you know God is in all of this? It will all be restored and be made new and we are all safe!" He was right. It was going to be okay.

Jake took on a whole new role for the house, not just a property manager but so much more since we were not there. He was our eyes, ears, and boots on the ground. He lined up all the meetings with insurance, retrofitting and restoring the damage, and construction at the house. He did crazy tasks like put tarps on our roof to protect it from the incoming storms when they were not secure because car-sized holes in our roof left our house exposed to the elements. Jake facilitated the packing and moving of the entire house; managing all the chaos of organizing destroyed items, items that needed to be cleaned, and items that needed to be stored off-site. He had to empty every cupboard, closet, and drawer in the entire house. It was a full-time job for weeks, but he excelled at it. Jake did an outstanding job coordinating all the contractors who needed to come through the house. We are deeply grateful for his help, especially since we couldn't have managed everything from Dallas. What a sweet and timely blessing from the Lord he has been to us.

Our family friends in San Diego have supported us in ways we never could have imagined. They took in the boys and fed them and became their point of stability by giving them a place to live for weeks. They say that fish and house guests begin to smell after three days. I am sure they began to really stink because they were there for weeks because they didn't have anywhere else to go. Finally, insurance approved a hotel for them to stay in.

I repeated the fact that all the boys were safe and how grateful I was for their safety. I was trying to change my mindset to focus on what was true and good. But after that initial Scripture, I didn't hear much from the Lord for a few months. I knew He would speak to me about the fire, and I knew I would know it was Him, so I continued to read His Word and study His teachings. I was seeking Him throughout my days with eyes wide open. I waited. And waited. And waited on the Lord. This is what I wrote in my journal:

> *Lord, I have been looking for You to speak to me. I have not heard from You, but I still feel You with me. Thank You for reminding me that I am not alone in this hard time. You love my family and care about all the details. I am still beyond thankful that You protected Jake and Luke and their friend. Lord, I want to hear from You. I want to not be so uneasy and fragile about this situation. Lord, help me to trust You more with the house.*

After closing my journal with a deep sigh, I decided to wander through a new Christian blog I'd just discovered. I wasn't searching for anything in particular, at least, that's what I thought. But God has a way of placing His words exactly where I need them. As I scrolled, my eyes caught on the sidebar, and there it was! Just like it had been waiting just for me. The words leapt from the screen:

> *There is another in the fire.*
> **DANIEL 3:25**

It was a direct word from heaven into my ordinary afternoon regarding the fire and my uneasy heart. I read it in awe. What? Was there someone in the fire? I needed to know more. God was involved in it. He was there in the fire. I could envision Him walking around and ushering the boys out of the house. I "saw" Him upstairs walking through our room and through the halls, making sure the precious photos on the walls were removed and stacked down in the garage. The firemen in our house actually did this for us. These firemen had hearts of gold. They also put tarps over our clothes to try and protect what they could from the flood of water they had to use to get the fire out.

The roof was destroyed and had three huge holes the size of Ford F-150s in them, and the chimney itself had fallen into our master closet. What was left of our ceiling in the bathroom and closet collapsed overnight. The sweetness of the situation was that the corner of my closet where my wedding dress was safely stored in a white box on the top shelf was not touched. When the ceiling fell down, it laid on the corner of the box and didn't even dent the box. God had spared my wedding dress. I know He did this, and it felt so personal.

God was there, and He verified it. This was what I had been waiting for, for Him to speak to me. The full verse says,

> *"Look!"* he answered, *"I see four men loose, walking*
> *in the midst of the fire; and they are not hurt, and*
> *the form of the fourth is like the Son of God."*
> DANIEL 3:25

My heart longed to hear that He was in it, that we weren't alone, and that He indeed allowed it like we had been saying. The peace that fell over me that I still feel today helped my heart understand and heal. I have this incredible peace that the Holy Spirit gave me. He reassured me He was there in our house during the fire. That unstable, weepy feeling I walked around with for weeks, I mean months, was gone. The Lord spoke to my heart and my soul, and I am shouting from the burned rooftops this time that He is God! I am literally smiling as I write this.

Let me next share some more great blessings that are straight from the Lord. After Ryan graduated from Baylor in the spring, he moved back to San Diego with his two brothers. Remember how I said in chapter 19 that the boys became best friends? This is still true today as they chose to live together. They have the best relationship, and my heart just smiles when I see them together. The boys are all in a rental house in a town called Cardiff-by-the-Sea. The blessing is that it is walking distance from the beach, and when the boys finish work, they go surf.

Michael and I came for a long visit during the summer and were able to enjoy our time together and this beach town. Pink and orange sunsets over the Pacific Ocean are painted in the skies almost every summer evening. My family has had the best summer, and we have been fortunate enough to live in rental properties close to the beach, which feels like a vacation every day of the week. It didn't matter what house we were in; we were cared for and blessed beyond what we ever thought we needed.

But most importantly, God has redeemed and done a great work in my heart. Throughout this whole process of losing my house and then knowing that God was in it the whole time and He protected my boys was more than I could have ever asked. I've learned that the house is just a house. The sweetness comes from God when He takes care of us whether our home is rebuilt or not. I had been holding onto "things" so tightly as if that is what sustains me. No wonder I felt wobbly and uneasy. I was holding onto my house as if it was my foundation. I needed to release it like we had done when we were going to sell it back in 2004. I needed to give it all to Him.

If our hands are clenched tight onto the things of the world, then how is God ever going to work in this situation? We must hold our hands out with our palms open, which feels like the most dangerous exercise, allowing God to take away old things and replace them with new blessings, trusting Him with it all. You might be stripped of something that you hold so dearly to your heart, but you will come out the other side feeling loved by the Creator of the world who provides for His children in a perfect way. Jon Courson said, "Perhaps sometimes we go through elongated difficulties and trials because, like Job, we're struggling to prove our point, to justify our position, or to have our way. But could it be that the Lord might say, 'Just die. Give it up. Lay it down'?"[14]

Maybe your house didn't burn like ours, but my guess is there is some hardship or pain in your life that you may be struggling with that has burned you and hurt you. Is it making you weepy, confused, and frustrated like I was feeling? Have you been wondering how this will ever turn around? The Lord is your answer, like He was for me. Open your hands and your heart and give it to Him. Let Him be your solution. Start hunting for His love, His words, His encouragement, His redemption, His way. God promises that when we seek Him, we will find Him when we search for Him with all our heart (Jeremiah 29:13). So together, let's continue hunting for honey that is sweeter than any sweetness we've known and more beautiful than anything we've ever imagined.

HONEY NUGGET

Even in the fiercest fires of life, God is with us in the flames, turning ashes into beauty and proving that His foundation will never crumble.

A NOTE FROM HEIDI

When I started writing *Hunting for Honey*, I didn't know the title or what my God stories would add up to in the end. However, I knew God had revealed Himself to me throughout my life in so many beautiful ways. I learned so much in this journey of seeking and finding Him, learning that it takes two to be in my relationship with Him. I had to be intentional, all the while expecting to find Him in every moment. Kind of like hunting: hunting for that perfect dress for an event or the perfect recipe to serve for your guests or, in my case, a "perfect match" for a date. The dress, the recipe, the date don't just appear. Rather, I had to do something. I had to start looking and go through the process. As my collection of stories grew, I saw that I had been anticipating and longing to hear, see, and experience God—all of His goodness and His kindness. That was the common thread that held these stories together to make this collection into thirty-two chapters of encounters with God. They are so sweet. Like drops of honey.

My hope is that as you read these stories, you found yourself nodding, smiling, maybe even tearing up, and sensing that same presence. That you saw a reflection of your own journey and started noticing God in your everyday life too. Whether you are in the wilderness or the middle of the promised land, He is with you.

I pray you keep seeking and finding God in your life, in the everyday and unexpected.

With all my love,
Heidi

P.S. I'd love to hear from you—
visit me at *www.heidigianni.com*

ACKNOWLEDGMENTS

To my husband, Michael, my steady rock and greatest encourager. You believed in me before I believed in myself. You did more than support me. You coached me, cheered me on, and walked beside me through every high and low of learning to write and publish this book. Thank you for the endless conversations we shared through every step. You have been my sounding board from morning to night. I could not have made it here without you. I love you, and I thank you.

To Jake, who said, "Mom, just start writing; you have something to say." Your words settled deep in my heart and echoed each time I faced a blank page. They came back to me again as I pushed through the hard work of shaping every story and reliving each moment. The conversations we shared about God, writing, and life gave me the courage and strength I needed to begin.

To Luke, who recognized how deeply God placed this calling on my heart and how important it was to me to write a book. You understood from the very beginning that writing this book mattered, not only for me but also for the purpose God intended. You were my constant voice, checking in and reminding me of the importance of seeing this through. Thank you for listening to me, for offering wisdom when I needed it most, and for always pointing me back to the truth.

To Ryan, thank you for pushing me to never quit, no matter how hard it was. You are the reason I had to finish. The way you live with determination and excellence inspired me to keep going. Our deep conversations and your wisdom always kept me thinking about my reader and who might need these stories. Your example of perseverance was the fuel that kept my fingers typing, even when I wanted to give up.

To Heather, my little sister who faithfully talked me through every roadblock and every lie that whispered, "No one would want to hear these stories." You were the one who first suggested I write a book. At first I thought the idea was crazy, and I pushed it aside for months, but you saw something I couldn't yet see. Now I know you were right. This was exactly what I was called to do. Thank you, Heather, for believing in me before I believed in myself.

To my Kleis Family 19, your love, support, and prayers were a constant comfort. I knew I could count on you to be cheering me on in every season of this process. Thank you for letting me use you as the canvas of so many of my stories. I am forever grateful for each of you and the life we share together.

To my lifelong, OG, best friends in San Diego, your advice, deep conversations, text messages, phone calls, and excitement were invaluable as I forged ahead with this idea. You girls are my biggest fans. My heart overflows with love and gratitude for each of you and "I thank my God upon every remembrance of you" (Philippians 1:3).

To my Texas Bible study, community group, and OG neighborhood mahjong and sourdough friends, thank you for all of your prayers and love. You literally walked with me through every twist and turn of this book: the title, the tagline, the cover, the edits. You lifted every detail in prayer and celebrated every milestone with me. You helped carry this dream. Thank you for every ounce of help you gave me.

To Lori Zimbardi, whom I met walking through the parking lot on our way to Bob Goff's Writers Workshop at The Oaks Retreat Center. That divine appointment turned into a beautiful friendship. You became my first reader, then my editor, my encourager, and my steady guide on this author's journey. You taught me so much by gently holding my hand. Thank you.

To Bob Goff, your Writing Room Podcast and Writer's Workshop in February of 2024, literally helped me understand how to write a book and publish it. I listened and relistened to every podcast to glean every ounce of wisdom and knowledge from you. Attending your Writer's Workshop was instrumental in writing this book. I appreciate every call and email we had. They were the fuel I needed to write this book. I am forever grateful for your wisdom and encouragement. And thank you for writing my endorsement. I am still smiling that you said yes.

To Pastor Rick Warren, author of the *Daily Hope* and former pastor of Saddleback Church who has filled me with so much wisdom and knowledge of the Lord with his daily emails, podcasts, and messages. Your teachings have always pointed me to Jesus and helped me live my life for Him. Thank you for all you have done in my life.

To my thematic editor Blair Parke and to my proofreader, LB. I can't thank you enough for all of the talent and expertise you used on my heap of words to make them shine and shimmer and make sense for the reader. I am so impressed with you both and your work.

To my cover designer, Vanessa Mendozzi, thank you for designing a cover that encompasses my heart for the book. I would have never thought I would have insects on my cover.

To my interior designer, Steve Kuhn, thank you for making my words look beautiful and organized on the pages. This makes my heart smile.

To Natalie Myers, my web designer and new friend, not only did you do a fabulous job on the website, but you also showed up for me where I needed it most. I didn't have any reviews or readers for the book at that early point, and you volunteered to read my stories to help me by being my first "review." That was so sweet. Thank you.

And last but not least, all glory and praise to God, our loving Father, His Son, Jesus, our Savior, and the Holy Spirit who led me to write this book.

With a heart full of gratitude,
Heidi

BIBLIOGRAPHY

Allen, Jennie. *Find Your People: Building Deep Community in a Lonely World.* Colorado Springs, CO: WaterBrook, 2023.

Cloud, Henry. *Trust: Knowing When to Give It, When to Withhold It, How to Earn It, and How to Fix It When It Gets Broken in Life and Business.* New York, NY: Worthy, 2023.

Courson, Jon. *Application Commentary Old Testament, Volume 1.* Nashville, TN: Thomas Nelson Inc., 2005.

Eldredge, John, and Stasi Eldredge. *Captivating: Unveiling the Mystery of a Woman's Soul, Expanded Edition.* Nashville, TN: Thomas Nelson, 2021.

Goff, Bob. *Everybody, Always: Becoming Love in a World Full of Setbacks and Difficult People.* Nashville, TN: Thomas Nelson, 2018.

Ortlund, Dane. *Gentle and Lowly: The Heart of Christ for Sinners and Sufferers.* Wheaton, IL: Crossway, 2020.

Warren, Rick. *The Purpose Driven Life: Expanded Edition.* Grand Rapids, MI: Zondervan, 2012.

NOTES

1. Henry Cloud, *Trust* (Worthy, 2023), 46.

2. Bob Goff, *Everybody, Always* (Thomas Nelson, 2018), 209.

3. John Eldredge and Stasi Eldredge, *Captivating* (Thomas Nelson, 2021), 115.

4. Ibid., 8.

5. Ibid., 115-116.

6. Ibid., 116.

7. Ibid., 117.

8. Rick Warren, *The Purpose Driven Life* (Zondervan, 2012), 22.

9. Dane Ortlund, *Gentle and Lowly* (Crossway, 2020), 122.

10. Ibid., 122.

11. Jon Courson, *Application Commentary Old Testament, Volume 1* (Thomas Nelson, 2005), 354.

12. Jon Courson, *Application Commentary Old Testament, Volume 1* (Thomas Nelson, 2005), 354.

13. Jennie Allen, *Find Your People* (WaterBrook, 2023), 134.

14. Jon Courson, *Application Commentary Old Testament, Volume 1* (Thomas Nelson, 2005), 1314.